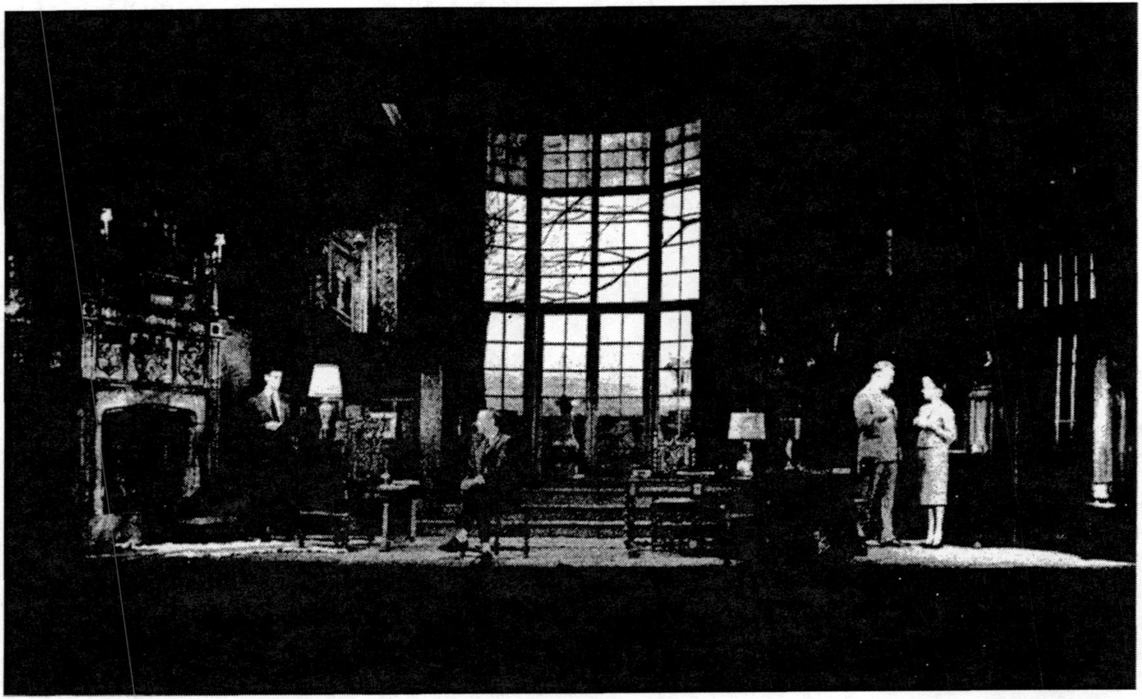

PHOTO BY GRAPHIC HOUSE

WRITE ME A MURDER

BY **FREDERICK KNOTT**

★

★

**DRAMATISTS
PLAY SERVICE
INC.**

WRITE ME A MURDER was first presented by Compass Productions, Inc., at the Belasco Theatre in New York City on October 26, 1961. It was directed by George Schaefer; the settings were by Warren Clymer; and the costumes by Noel Taylor. The cast, in order of appearance, was as follows:

THE HON. CLIVE RODINGHAM .... Denholm Elliot
DR. ELIZABETH WOOLLEY .... Ethel Griffies
THE HON. DAVID RODINGHAM .... James Donald
CHARLES STURROCK .... Torin Thatcher
JULIE STURROCK .... Kim Hunter
MR. TIBBIT, THE BUILDER .... Robert Milli
CONSTABLE HACKETT .... Herbert Voland
TWO MEN .... John D. Irving, Robert Milli

SYNOPSIS OF SCENES

The action of the play takes place in Rodingham Manor,
about two hours from London.

ACT ONE

SCENE 1: A winter morning.
SCENE 2: A week later. Afternoon.
SCENE 3: Two hours later.
SCENE 4: Three weeks later. Night.

ACT TWO

SCENE 1: The following evening.
SCENE 2: About a year later. Night.
SCENE 3: Several weeks later. Late afternoon.

ACT THREE

SCENE 1: The same evening.
SCENE 2: Early the following morning.

3

WRITE ME A MURDER

ACT ONE

SCENE 1

PLACE: *The library and study of Rodingham Manor.*
(For description of the set, see separate notes)
It is bright and sunny outside. In the library, Clive Rod-
ingham is telephoning. He is 30 to 35, attractively aristo-
cratic, and well aware of it.

CLIVE. May I speak to Mr. Charles Sturrock? . . . Oh! . . .
Then would you tell him Clive Rodingham phoned—and that my
father is still very ill—so could he come here . . . perhaps some
day next week instead? . . . Thank you. (*He hangs up. While
he is speaking, Dr. Elizabeth Woolley comes down the stairs, carrying her bag. She puts this on the round side table. She is a very
old, no-nonsense country doctor, the kind that never retires.*) How
is he?
WOOLLEY. (*Cheerfully.*) Still sleeping. I might as well be giving
you that vaccination. Sit down. (*As they talk, Clive rolls up his
sleeve, sits in chair A, and She gives him a vaccination.*) Clive, as
I brought you into the world, might I be allowed one personal
question?
CLIVE. As many as you like, Liz.
WOOLLEY. Are you *really* in love with her?
CLIVE. I tell you she's the most natural and adorably spontane-
ous . . .
WOOLLEY. Now don't be evasive! I am speaking as your family
physician. I am referring to plain animal attraction. And it's as
simple as this: Will this young heiress be able to torture the very
hell out of you, simply by saying "no?" Because if she can't, you'll
soon take her for granted. And whenever *you* take a girl for
granted, she's miserable within a week. And if any man thinks

5

he can live happily with a miserable woman, he's an idiot. And that goes for horses, dogs, pigs, geese and Rodinghams. Especially Rodinghams. (*Finishing the vaccination.*) There! Now you are immune to smallpox . . . but not to the vengeance of a woman scorned. (*As she puts her instruments away in bag Clive rises and puts on jacket.*)

CLIVE. Thank you, Liz. Glass of sherry?

WOOLLEY. No thanks, but I've been dying for a smoke all morning. Got a light? (*As she digs in her doctor's bag and finds cigarettes.*) I hope David isn't too late.

CLIVE. (*Lighting her cigarette.*) I doubt if he'll turn up. Lives on this old houseboat up the Thames. I suppose they deliver telegrams to houseboats.

WOOLLEY. It must be almost fifteen years.

CLIVE. Yes, he'd find the old place a bit jaded, I'm afraid. But then he never cared too much for Rodingham.

WOOLLEY. He *adored* this place. Far more than you ever did. I remember driving him around the village the day before he left with his mother. He was only fifteen, but even then he was—full of plans. (*Sits, chair D.*)

CLIVE. Oh yes, David was always very go-ahead . . . surprised he never went further. Just lives alone on this houseboat writing nasty little stories . . . (*Sits chair B. David appears on the terrace riding his bicycle from L. He alights and leans it against the balustrade. He wears a duffle coat over sport clothes and slings a knapsack. David is about two years younger than Clive and, in character, a complete contrast. He is quiet and gentle in manner and has none of Clive's arrogance.*)

WOOLLEY. They're not nasty at all, Clive. Ingenious and rather amusing . . . a little gruesome sometimes. But then he has to earn a living somehow so why shouldn't he write. (*David disappears R.*)

CLIVE. Well—how would you like your *only* daughter to marry into a very old English family, only to discover that her brother-in-law lives like a hermit writing nasty little stories? Twist that a bit and he's a Socialist and a sex fiend. (*The front door slams shut. Clive turns, sees David in hall, rises and greets him as he enters.*) Ah David! Welcome home!

DAVID. Hello Clive . . . Liz!

WOOLLEY. (*Warmly.*) David! (*They embrace.*)

6

DAVID. How's father?

WOOLLEY. (*Quite cheerfully.*) Not good. I think it might be today. Glad you were able to come. (*The Nurse calls anxiously from upstairs.*)

NURSE. (*Off.*) Doctor!

WOOLLEY. (*Calmly, stubbing out her cigarette.*) All right, I'm coming, Nurse! . . . When he's awake you can come up and see him. Meanwhile—try not to kill each other. (*She pauses in hall doorway.*) Oh, and just to start you off—Clive is going to sell Rodingham, emigrate, and marry an American with . . . (*As she goes up the stairs with bag.*) six Cadillacs . . . only two airplanes . . . but four helicopters . . . and heaven knows how many millions . . . (*Disappears.*)

DAVID. You're selling Rodingham!

CLIVE. David, when your only brother is about to be married, you could show *some* interest—or at least pretend to.

DAVID. Congratulations, Clive.

CLIVE. Thank you, David.

DAVID. How long have you known—this one?

CLIVE. Met her with her mother at St. Moritz. Taught her to ski.

DAVID. May she present you with a male heir at the earliest opportunity.

CLIVE. Well, as she has six brothers, there's rather more than a chance. And as it happens . . . (*As they talk, David looks around sadly at the faded condition of his old home.*)

DAVID. (*Interrupting.*) Are you selling just the house or . . . ?

CLIVE. The land, the village, everything. At least I hope to. Remember Charlie Sturrock who used to work at Wollock's Groceries?

DAVID. The big fellow? Red face?

CLIVE. That's right. And always sweating! Only he isn't a grocery boy any longer. Buys and sells everything from scrap iron to office buildings. And now he wants Rodingham!

DAVID. But has father agreed to this?

CLIVE. (*Sits in chair A.*) Now there was obviously no point in telling *him*. In fact, Sturrock has been trying to buy the place for years. But you know father. Then last week he approached me in London, rather craftily, wined me and dined me and made a tentative offer: "In anticipation," as he put it. And of course, father's leaving Rodingham to me. (*A pause, as he lights cigarette.*) You

7

do understand, don't you? It has always been left to the eldest son. For over five hundred years.

DAVID. (*Crossing to study.*) Yes, but for over five hundred years —no eldest son has ever sold it, has he? (*David goes into study. He examines the new wall for a moment and then looks through the window at Rodingham village. As they talk, David discards his coat on study chair.*)

CLIVE. Your point is well taken, David, but unfortunately we must move with the times.

DAVID. (*Calling to the other room.*) Do you have to let the village go? Why not one of the farms?

CLIVE. (*Calling back.*) We've sold most of them already. We're down to four hundred acres.

DAVID. Keep Hill?

CLIVE. Keep Hill, Longmeadow, Birchfields . . .

DAVID. (*Returning to the library.*) Longmeadow! That was the best land we had.

CLIVE. (*Amused.*) Oh come off it, David. You've got to be a realist these days. (*As he goes to sideboard and pours himself sherry.*) The reign of the country squire is over. Father was lucky. He at least got in for the tail end.

DAVID. There was never a better way of living invented.

CLIVE. (*Crossing to writing table with his glass.*) Oh, I know! Horses, dogs and the gentle English countryside as one's playground! But poke around in the foundations and you'll soon find that all this was as solidly based on *finance* as a city bank. (*Sits on the edge of table.*) You've been well out of it these last few years!

DAVID. You'll get some kind of job in America?

CLIVE. I suppose so. Yes.

DAVID. Such as?

CLIVE. Now don't be dense, David. The girl's mother has eighty million dollars. She'll find me *something* to do!

DAVID. I'm sure she will! (*Pause.*) I wish I was a realist.

CLIVE. Well you aren't and you never will be. And now you *are* here—how long can you stay?

DAVID. (*Sits chair A.*) I'm not staying. I just wanted to see father once.

CLIVE. Wish you could hang around here for a bit. Just until Sturrock moves in. You see I'd like to get over there just as soon

8

as—as soon as possible. She keeps phoning me every day from Texas to "hurry on out!"

DAVID. What's she like?

CLIVE. (Bewildered.) Hmm?

DAVID. I said—what's she like?

CLIVE. (Suddenly realizing that he means his fiance.) Oh, perfection! You know, these Americans are really remarkable. She's exquisitely feminine. And yet she can swim like a fish and skis like a bird.

DAVID. I thought you taught her to ski?

CLIVE. Oh, that was the mother.

DAVID. Oh! And which one phones you every day from Texas . . . ?

CLIVE. The mother but . . .

DAVID. But it is the daughter you're going to marry?

CLIVE. It is indeed!

DAVID. Ah!

CLIVE. (Rises.) And incidentally, David, when are you going to give some thought to marriage? (Pause.)

DAVID. When I meet her I'll give it my undivided attention.

CLIVE. Take my tip. Choose from the girls with something of their own. Though you may have difficulty getting her aboard that houseboat. I never met a rich girl who could sleep in a hammock.

DAVID. I have no wish to start imitating father . . .

CLIVE. And what exactly would you mean by that?

DAVID. Well? Why do you think he married her?

CLIVE. (Loudly.) And this is a hell of a day to bring that up! (Woolley comes halfway down the stairs and calls from "the portal.")

WOOLLEY. Boys! Boys! Your father's awake now . . . May not be for long. (Sound of Rolls coming up drive. Clive and David start towards the stairs, then Clive notices something through the window.)

CLIVE. Oh, Lord! Here comes Sturrock in his bloody great Rolls! . . . Hey, David! Get your damned bike out of the way!

WOOLLEY. (On landing.) You didn't invite him today!

CLIVE. You said you never expected father to last out the weekend . . . (David exits by library window, and takes his bicycle off L.)

9

WOOLLEY. But you could have stopped him! (*Comes down the stairs, enters Library.*)

CLIVE. I phoned his office, but they must have . . .

WOOLLEY. Upstairs! Both of you. I'll handle young Charlie. (*Charles and Julie pass library window on way to the front door.*)

CLIVE. No, I'll have to see him now.

WOOLLEY. (*Crossing to fireplace.*) I whipped out his adenoids when he was seven. Since then he's turned pale at the sight of me. (*Doorbell rings. David re-enters through Library windows, stands above chair C. Clive opens front door. Then, as Charles and Julie enter hall:*)

CLIVE. (*With all his charm.*) Ah! Good morning! Do come in.

CHARLES. (*In hall.*) Morning. This is my wife. Lord Rodingham. (*Clive takes Charles' hat, drops it on bench in hall.*)

CLIVE and JULIE. (*In hall.*) How do you do. (*Charles, Julie and Clive enter Library, in that order. Charles is 45 to 50, shrewd and a very live-wire. He shows flashes of humor and has that hard won dignity of the self-made-man. He is dressed today as a businessman. Julie is 25 to 30, gentle, introspective, and when Charles is around, rather mousy.*)

CLIVE. You remember my brother David?

CHARLES. (*Crossing to David.*) Yes, indeed! (*Shakes hands.*) Julie . . . Mr. David Rodingham.

DAVID. How do you do.

JULIE. How do you—how do you do. (*Charles glances quickly from one to the other.*)

CHARLES. You two haven't met before, have you?

DAVID. I don't believe. . . .

JULIE. I think . . . I've read some of your stories.

DAVID. Oh, I see. (*Doctor Woolley moves to Charles from behind and taps him on the back. He turns.*)

CHARLES. (*Noisily.*) Well! Look who's here! (*Shakes hands.*) You haven't changed a bit. This is my wife, Julie—Dr. Woolley.

WOOLLEY. How do you do?

JULIE. How do you do.

CHARLES. (*Loudly.*) Well! Some water's gone under the bridge since . . .

WOOLLEY. (*Quietly.*) Charlie! Sorry to interrupt, but Lord Rodingham is upstairs. And he just woke up . . .

CHARLES. He *what!*

10

WOOLLEY. (*Crossing to stairs.*) So we're going up to see him . . .

CHARLES. (*Turning to Clive, almost angrily.*) But I thought you said . . . !

CLIVE. (*With ease and charm.*) It's perfectly all right . . . You see, my father made the most remarkable recovery last week-end. We won't keep you very long, if you don't mind waiting.

JULIE. Please don't worry about us. (*David and Woolley are going up the stairs.*)

CLIVE. (*To Julie.*) May I offer you a glass of sherry?

CHARLES. Never touch it, thanks.

CLIVE. No, of course you don't. Mrs. Sturrock?

JULIE. No, thank you.

CLIVE. Then I'll join you in a few minutes. (*When Clive has disappeared upstairs.*)

JULIE. (*In a whisper.*) We really ought to go! (*Charles takes off overcoat, throws it onto chair A.*)

CHARLES. Nonsense. His fault for not telling us in time. (*As though delighted, looking around the room.*) Well! This is in a worse mess than I thought! (*As he talks he moves about, prodding and kicking the furniture, as if he was examining a second-hand car. He peeps through the kitchen door. Julie looks at rest of house through window.*)

JULIE. But it's enormous!

CHARLES. That's right. Play that up. It's too big for you to run.

JULIE. Well, it is, isn't it? In any case, we can't even go upstairs today. Why not come back another time?

CHARLES. Because this one calls for a bit of hustling. I've been keeping tabs on young Master Clive. He wants to sell this fast so he can join his rich fiancee in America. So just watch me knock him down ten thousand! (*He moves towards study, then pauses.*) Now there's something wrong here! Why did they put this wall up? This used to be one room. (*He slaps study wall.*) It's only plywood.

JULIE. Do you really want all this? And you know how you hate drafts. (*Charles has entered study and is staring at the electric stove.*)

CHARLES. (*With glee.*) That's it! Look, look, look! His little stove! (*Julie enters study.*) His Lordship couldn't afford to heat the whole room so he built himself this little place to keep warm

11

in in the winter! So he could sit by this window and contemplate his village. (*He looks through window.*) And how's this for a view —eh? (*Julie looks through window.*) See that black and white cottage, left of the church? That's where I was born. And that's the blasted hill I had to pedal up a hundred times a week. And over that other hill is the Duke's village. Everybody has his own village around here. Isn't that nice? (*He goes back into the library and points at the portrait above fireplace. Julie follows.*) Now there's the *first* Baron Rodingham. He was a gangster. Did some dirty work for Edward the Fourth. They've been living off him for five hundred years. (*Pointing at fourth wall.*) And that's the *fourteenth* baron, the man upstairs.

JULIE. Their father?

CHARLES. Their father. He was born at the right time, he was. There were house parties here every weekend. And twenty servants wasn't enough to clean up afterwards. So I used to come up here myself and make a few bob . . . You see, his Lordship was exactly like Clive—only more so. Their mother was a rich woman when he married her. And when this place had soaked up every penny she had, he sacked her with the rest of the servants. But he had to let her take David in order to keep Clive. (*Sits at writing table, chair C.*) All he wanted was an heir to his realm. So David became a sort of poor relation. You say he's a writer?

JULIE. Yes, I've read quite a few of his stories. They're rather clever.

CHARLES. You know we could *use* Mr. David. Take you around and introduce you to the local gentry? Better you than me, I fancy . . . (*During the above, Clive and David come quietly down the stairs.*)

JULIE. (*To warn him.*) Charles!

CLIVE. Thank you so much for waiting. Now where would you like to begin? The kitchen and servants' quarters are through there. (*He points to kitchen door, but tries to lead Charles into the hall.*) And the dining hall and ballroom are *this* way . . . (*Charles rises and turns to David, ignoring Clive.*)

CHARLES. I hadn't realized you were an author, Mr. Rodingham. My wife's a bit of a writer herself, or hopes to be.

DAVID. Oh, really?

CHARLES. Wish you'd give her some tips sometime. She hasn't

12

quite got the knack yet. How long does it take you to write a story?

DAVID. Well, it depends. About two weeks.

CHARLES. (*To Julie.*) See? What did I tell you? (*To David.*) She takes two weeks a page! (*To Clive.*) Come on, then, let's leave these two scribes together. I'll look at the drainage first. (*Charles opens library window and leads Clive to terrace. Clive pauses to point out the sundial, but Charles appears disinterested and they move off* L.)

JULIE. We're so very sorry . . . about our coming here today.

DAVID. Oh, that's quite all right. Won't you sit down?

JULIE. Oh, thank you. (*She sits in chair* A. *David takes Charles' coat to bench in hall and then goes to fireplace. She looks around the room.*) This is really very old, isn't it?

DAVID. Yes it is. (*Pointing up at first Baron.*) He built it in 1478. But of course it wasn't always like this, it's been burned down three times. Have you seen the village yet?

JULIE. Only from the window, in there. If you half close your eyes it's like being back hundreds of years.

DAVID. Yes, we've always tried to keep it that way. We think it's the most unspoiled village in England. Have you ever lived in the country?

JULIE. Oh yes, our home was in Cornwall, but we had to sell it when my father died and then I went to London.

DAVID. Oh, I see. (*Pause.*) And you write . . . novels?

JULIE. Just short stories. At least I write them, but they don't print them. I've written over twenty in seven years and not a single one.

DAVID. Then you *must* be a writer! I'd have given up long before that. Do you ever—show your stories to anyone?

JULIE. Only my agent. Perhaps you know him—Paul Weiner?

DAVID. No, I don't.

JULIE. Of course he's hardly *my* agent because he never gets any commission, but he's been a good friend to me and tells me what's wrong . . . like this. (*She hands him a small note from her purse.*)

DAVID. (*Reading.*) Julie—Characters excellent as always, but *where's the story?* Paul! (*Laughs and hands it back. As he crosses above chair* A *to writing table and turns.*) Well, now you know! I'm the other way 'round. It just amuses me to work out a plot.

13

You should try a murder story some time. Good exercise in construction.

JULIE. As a matter of fact, I'm writing one now. . . . I suppose you couldn't . . . read it sometime?

DAVID. I'd like to—very much.

JULIE. I'd be terribly grateful. . . . Should I post it . . . here?

DAVID. No, I live on a houseboat . . . (*Hesitates.*) at least I *am* planning to stay on here, for the next few weeks. That is, unless you decide to move in right away. . . . (*Charles' voice can be heard from kitchen.*)

JULIE. Oh, I don't think we'll do that. I mean—this is really far too big for us. You see, we've been living in hotels ever since we were married and . . . (*Charles and Clive enter from kitchen.*)

CHARLES. . . . Well, there you are, you see. Your father should have sold it to me before the rot set in. . . .

CLIVE. But you haven't even begun to look at it yet. . . .

CHARLES. I've seen all I need. It's the cost of those repairs. And the lawns are hayfields. The kitchen garden's a jungle. . . . (*To Julie.*) Well, dear? Would it break your heart if I said "no"?

JULIE. (*Rises.*) It wouldn't, I'm afraid. I was just explaining to Mr. Rodingham . . . (*Charles turns to Clive with a sad smile.*)

CHARLES. You see! So we won't waste your time any longer. And I'm sorry we turned up at the wrong moment, as it were. Did I leave my coat . . . ?

DAVID. I'll get it for you. (*Fetches coat from hall.*)

CLIVE. Mr. Sturrock. I'm prepared to consider a lower figure if . . . (*As David returns and helps Charles on with his coat.*)

CHARLES. All I could give you is a flat price. Say . . . Oh, I dunno . . . fifty for the lot? And you throw in the wine cellar and everything.

CLIVE. *Fifty* thousand! The wine cellar alone is worth three thousand. And you're not forgetting the four hundred acres?

CHARLES. Is that all? I thought you said five hundred. (*Laughs.*) Sorry, Mr. Rodingham. (*To Julie.*) Ready, dear?

CLIVE. What do you mean by—everything?

CHARLES. The lot! Everything I may want—in the whole house.

CLIVE. Everything you may want? That's not very specific, is it?

CHARLES. Oh, you want me to be specific? All right! In the kitchen—nothing! You can sling that out. But in the rest of the house—everything, just as it stands. (*Pointing at fourth wall.*)

14

Those books, portraits. All the carpets, curtains . . . (*He goes into the study. Clive follows.*) And in this room, those guns and everything on the walls . . . (*He picks up silver cigarette box from desk.*) And this. . . .

WOOLLEY. (*Who started down the stairs during Charles' speech —and is now in the hall doorway.*) Is Clive there? (*David crosses to the study.*)

CLIVE. (*To Charles.*) Aren't you asking rather a lot for fifty thousand . . . ?

CHARLES. (*Raising his voice.*) And I may say—the holes in the roof, the trees that are growing in through the windows and the cockroaches in the kitchen and don't tell me there aren't any because . . . ! (*David has entered study.*)

DAVID. Excuse me, Mr. Sturrock . . . Clive.

CLIVE. Excuse me. (*Clive follows David into the library. Woolley comes to them and puts a hand on each of their shoulders and whispers something. Meanwhile Julie, realizing the situation, goes quietly into study and closes door. In the study: Charles listens at door, then turns to Julie and whispers excitedly.*)

CHARLES. He's dead!

JULIE. (*Desperately.*) Then we must go!

CHARLES. Hold your ground. I've nearly got him! (*In the library:*)

WOOLLEY. . . . Nurse will stay until Mr. Willis arrives. I'll ask him to make all the arrangements. Funeral the day after tomorrow if that suits you? Now don't bother to see me out. (*She moves to hall.*) Where are the Sturrocks?

DAVID. They're in here. (*He crosses to study. Woolley enters. David closes door.*)

WOOLLEY. (*To the Sturrocks.*) Well—I'll say goodbye now. (*Quietly but cheerfully.*) Lord Rodingham has just died. (*Then louder.*) Nice to have seen you again, Charlie. (*Then to Julie.*) And if you decide to live here I shall expect to be the first to come to dinner.

CHARLES. (*Warmly.*) Well that's a promise! (*Then loudly, through closed door, for Clive's benefit.*) Though it won't be this house, I'm afraid! It's far too big for Mrs. Sturrock. And she makes the decisions in this family. (*Woolley turns slowly and looks at Charles.*)

WOOLLEY. Now come off it Charlie! (*As she exits by study*

15

French window.) You can't fool me! (*As Charles and Julie whisper in the study, Clive and David talk in the library. David is looking out of window. Clive is standing with his back to the fireplace.*)

CLIVE. Fifty thousand pounds . . . !

DAVID. (*Turning.*) Clive . . . !

CLIVE. What with debts and taxes—this will hardly leave me twenty thousand!

DAVID. Clive, don't sell. If you do we'll never get it back. I'll get you more than this.

CLIVE. (*Surprised.*) Where from?

DAVID. I don't know, but give me six months! I'll raise it some-how. . . .

CLIVE. (*With a laugh.*) Steady, David, steady . . . ! (*Angrily.*) And why the hell does he want the wine cellar? He doesn't even drink! (*The Sturrocks enter the library.*)

JULIE. (*To David, quietly.*) We're so sorry.

DAVID. Thank you.

CHARLES. (*To Julie, as he crosses to hall.*) If we hurry I can make that board meeting after all. . . .

CLIVE. Mr. Sturrock, I'll take fifty without the wine cellar. Frankly, I'd sooner give that away than sell it to anyone who—might not appreciate it.

CHARLES. My friends would appreciate it. It's with the wine or nothing. Come on, Julie. . . .

CLIVE. (*Wearily.*) All right, then, with the cellar. (*Charles halts in doorway, then turns.*)

CHARLES. Subject to contract and survey, of course.

CLIVE. Of course. (*As though he could not bear to watch this, David goes quietly into the study. He goes to window and stares down, very sadly, at the village of Rodingham. Charles takes a typed letter and a copy from his pocket.*)

CHARLES. Then if you'll just sign this and fill in the amount. . . . And there's a copy for you. (*Clive glances at letter as he crosses to writing table.*)

CLIVE. I'm not sure I'm entitled to sign this. . . .

CHARLES. (*Briskly.*) It's perfectly legal. Just an option. Your solicitor can send me the deeds and the contracts. (*Clive sits at writing table. Charles in chair B and takes out cheque book.*) I'll be giving you my cheque for the deposit. (*As he writes it out.*) You

16

know . . . Lord Rodingham . . . it's really a pity this wasn't done two years ago.

CLIVE. (*With all the superiority he can muster.*) Of course we're sorry to have kept you waiting, Mr. Sturrock. But then we have been here . . . five hundred years. (*Clive signs the letter and hands it to Charles. Charles tears out his cheque and hands it to Clive. During Clive's last speech Julie has moved quietly into the Study. For a moment or two she watches David by the window. She is full of sympathy for him. Then David turns and as they look straight at each other—*)

CURTAIN

AUDIO BRIDGE

(*The following phone conversation (recorded) is played over the loudspeaker system while the curtain is down between Scenes 1 and 2, of Act 1.*)
(*Sound of phone ringing.*)

DAVID. Rodingham one two. (*Charles is heard on the other end speaking briskly and very fast. David, slowly.*)

CHARLES. Lord Rodingham?

DAVID. No, this is David Rodingham. My brother's . . .

CHARLES. Sturrock here. How are things going?

DAVID. Fine. They've just started working on your bedroom. . . .

CHARLES. I'm coming down tomorrow to see the kitchen. Will your brother be there?

DAVID. No, he left for America, yesterday, but I can show you around. . . .

CHARLES. Good enough. Now there's something else—my wife sent you a story she wrote.

DAVID. Yes, I think it's very good. . . .

CHARLES. Did you see about that short story competition in one of the evening papers?

DAVID. No, I don't think I . . .

CHARLES. Closes in about three weeks and they publish the winners. Now how would you like to brush this one up for her and send it in? (*A pause.*)

DAVID. I don't quite understand. . . .

CHARLES. (*Impatiently.*) Look, I'm only trying to kick in the door for her. Once she gets into print she'll be all set.

DAVID. Well, she writes far better than I do. I don't mind talking it over with her if that's any help, but . . .

CHARLES. That's the idea! First prize is only a few pounds, but I'll see you aren't out of pocket. I'll bring her with me tomorrow. Oh! and tell the builders not to touch the kitchen until I've had a word with them. . . . (*As Charles' Voice is faded out, Curtain rises on Scene 2.*)

ACT ONE

Scene 2

TIME: *A week later. Afternoon.*

ALTERATIONS TO SET: *In Library: On sideboard is an electric kettle and tea set, for three. Library curtains are open and it is light outside. The fire is not burning.*

In Study: The curtains are closed and only the desk lamp is switched on. On floor below desk is a large paper carrier bag on which is printed WOLLOCK'S GROCERIES, LTD., RODINGHAM. *The silencer-pistol has been taken down from the wall and lies, still in its frame, on the desk. The small chest has been pulled away from left wall so we can see David's bang-contraption hanging down behind it (as in diagram B-1). On the chest is a small hammer.*

ON RISE: *David is in Library. He switches on tea kettle, takes soda siphon from sideboard and enters Study, then he squirts soda water over the carpet beneath bang-contraption. Sound of car approaching, car doors banging, etc. David quickly puts siphon on chest and moves chest back about three inches from wall (i.e. so that bang-contraption is now hidden behind it.) He then hides grocery bag behind the open Study door. While he is doing this, Charles and Julie cross Library window outside and then front doorbell rings. Instead of answering it, David picks up hammer and stands by other pistol frames. Doorbell rings again. David does not move. A few moments later Charles*

18

and Julie enter by front door. Charles is now dressed in very new tweeds and looks terribly "county." He is in a very good mood today. As they enter he says to Julie:

CHARLES. So you pick his brains about that story. And whatever you do, get some kind of introduction to the Duke.

JULIE. Yes, I won't forget.

CHARLES. (*As he crosses to the study, he tosses his cap on the library desk.*) Ah! There you are! Thought there was nobody in.

DAVID. Oh, I'm sorry. This frame was a bit loose. Do you mind passing . . . ? (*Charles takes the frame with the pistol from the study desk and gives it to David.*) Thank you. (*David hangs it up carefully.*)

JULIE. (*Coming into the study.*) I'm sorry we're late. It was all my fault.

CHARLES. (*Taking off his coat, returns to Library and throws it over chair C.*) Yes it was! Coming through the Duke's village she turns into a one-way street, if you please, and then takes half an hour to back out. (*David has picked up the silver cigarette box from the study desk. He now offers it to Julie.*)

JULIE. No, thank you. (*Charles is back in the study. David offers him a cigarette, but he dismisses it with a wave of his hand.*) I never seem to notice those road signs unless . . .

DAVID. (*Puts box back on desk.*) Nor do I. There's a new one way street in our vil . . .

CHARLES. (*Interrupting, to Julie.*) You don't notice them because you're looking at the road all the time. You're supposed to keep your eyes moving, watching out for people and cars behind, and signs that say '*One-Way Street'* !

JULIE. Well, I do try but . . .

CHARLES. But you try too hard! Like everything else you do, you're too tense. (*To David.*) She's what I call an 'almost person.' She's almost a good cook. She was almost a damned good secretary once. And she can almost write. (*He fishes a paper clipping from his pocket and hands it to David.*) Which reminds me, here's that competition I was telling you about.

DAVID. (*Reading it.*) Oh yes, I checked up on this. They hold it every year. (*The electric kettle begins to whistle in Library.*) Would you like some tea? (*As they follow David into Library.*)

CHARLES. No. I haven't time for that. Is the builder here yet?

DAVID. Yes, he's looking at your bedroom. (*David switches off kettle.*)

CHARLES. (*Going to the fireplace.*) Good, so you write that story now. I'll just give you a few ideas to start you off, if you like.

JULIE. (*To David.*) May I help?

DAVID. It's all right thanks. (*As David makes the tea, Julie takes off her coat and throws it over chair B.*)

CHARLES. (*As he crosses below the furniture to the R. of the library writing table.*) And so . . . This is a story about a business tycoon, who might be me. And he has a rival he wants out of the way . . . and so he finally decides that the only thing to do is to . . .

JULIE. (*Quietly.*) He has read it, Charles.

CHARLES. Look, you'll have your say in a moment. You can talk all afternoon.

JULIE. I'm sorry. (*David brings tea tray to the round table between chairs A and B.*)

CHARLES. So he . . .

DAVID. Could you move that, please? (*Julie moves ash tray from round table and puts it on sideboard.*)

CHARLES. (*Irritated.*) All finished? (*Pause, as David sits chair A, Julie chair B.*) So he decides to kill him. . . . Now if I were you I'd start from scratch. *You're* the business rival, Mr. Rodingham, and *I'm* going to kill you. Tonight! So we invite you to dinner. . . . But *before* you arrive I've rigged up my study so it appears to have been burgled and I've put on a large pair of shoes and made footprints all over my study and across the garden. . . . (*He makes his point by stumping across to fireplace.*)

DAVID. (*To Julie.*) Yes, I liked the shoes!

CHARLES. My idea, you know.

DAVID. Oh, was it?

CHARLES. (*To Julie.*) Didn't I say, "Why don't you make him wear an extra large pair of shoes?"

JULIE. Yes, you did.

CHARLES. (*To David.*) She gets a lot of her ideas from me. By the way, not a word of this to anyone! Hmmm? Let someone else get an idea like that and he'd write it up before she could type page one.

DAVID. Not a word.

CHARLES. And so you arrive for dinner, Mr. Rodingham. And

then . . . when no one is looking . . . I take you into my study and knock you on the head. All right?

DAVID. All right . . . so far.

CHARLES. And then it all goes to pieces. I mean my wife has to tell the police that while we were at dinner you went into the study alone! . . . (*Laughs.*) Well, that's no good! Who's going to believe her? (*Mr. Tibbit, the Builder, appears on the stairs and hovers impatiently.*)

DAVID. Yes, I think we need something better than that. (*Rising and crossing towards study.*) As a matter of fact, I have an idea which might fit in rather well. You remember when you came in just now I was in there fixing . . .

CHARLES. (*Shouts to Tibbit.*) All right, Mr. Tibbit, I can see you. (*To David.*) Well, I've got a hundred things to look at so I can't do *all* this for you. . . .

DAVID. I think we can get round that . . .

CHARLES. (*Going to hall.*) See what I mean? Now you don't have to win first prize. Just as long as it's published. (*To Tibbit, as he goes upstairs.*) Come on then, quick look at the bedroom, then the cottages . . . (*Charles and Tibbit disappear upstairs. Julie pours tea and hands to David.*)

JULIE. Milk and sugar?

DAVID. Thank you. Of course he's right about the alibi. The police would never believe you. What you need is one extra guest who is going to witness the crime. . . . Someone they couldn't possibly suspect . . . the local bank manager or . . .

JULIE. Or that doctor who was here the other day . . . ?

DAVID. (*Laughs.*) Liz Woolley! The very girl. Incorruptible and terrifyingly observant.

JULIE. But that's no good! If anyone sees Charles follow you into the study . . .

DAVID. Now wait a minute! This is a trick. The doctor will be *watching* all right. But she *won't* see it! Now you're going to do all the writing. I'll just give you this one idea and you can take it from there.

JULIE. Just a second then. (*She takes a pad and pencil from her handbag and as they talk, makes notes.*) Right.

DAVID. Now suppose it was in *this* house. You and Charles invite this business rival to dinner . . .

JULIE. That's you.

21

DAVID. That's me. You also invite the village doctor. So we arrive together and join Charles—who is in his study . . . hanging one of those pistols back on the wall . . . (*David is now standing in open study door. He has left his tea cup on writing table.*)

JULIE. Like you were doing just now . . . ?

DAVID. Exactly. And as we talk in there, he offers us a cigarette from that silver box . . . (*Julie stops taking notes and looks at David, curiously, as he strolls back into centre of library.*) And then he brings us back in here and gives us a drink. . . . Then *you* come downstairs. You say you've just seen a man lurking in the garden. . . .

JULIE. A *big* man.

DAVID. A big man. So Charles phones the police. Now it will take them at least ten minutes to arrive, so while we're waiting, Charles takes me back in there. (*Points to study.*)

JULIE. Why?

DAVID. Oh, I don't know. . . . He wants to check a clause in a contract or something. (*David moves to the study door again. Julie starts to follow.*) No, no! You stay in here with the doctor. That's your job: To prevent her from going in there. Now I'll be Charles. I won't be long, so just stay there and listen, very carefully. . . . (*Julie sits. As David goes into the study he turns as though speaking to someone.*) Come on, Mr. Rodingham. Let's get this bit of business over with . . .

IN STUDY:

(*Once in the study, David goes through the following actions very quickly and surely as though they have been well rehearsed. And as he does this he mumbles quietly to himself, as though two people were talking to each other. The audience need not hear what he is actually saying.*)

1. He *nearly* closes door.

2. He takes silencer-pistol from frame and returns to the door.

IN LIBRARY:

(*Just as the door is kicked shut, Charles and Tibbit come down-*

22

Then he fires the pistol (blank cartridge) towards the desk and at the same time he kicks the door shut fairly hard. The 'pfft' from the silencer is completely drowned by the slamming of the door.

3. He picks up the grocery bag from below desk and drops pistol into it.

4. He goes to desk and opens two of the drawers. He takes out some papers and scatters them on the floor.

5. He takes silver cigarette box from desk and drops it into bag.
6. He goes to wall and drops the remaining three pistols into grocery bag, one by one.

7. He opens the French window, but leaves the curtains drawn closed.
8. He hides grocery bag just outside window.

9. He hauls up bang-contraption from behind the chest. He lights the cigarette which is already attached to it. (*It is now in view of the audience, as in diagram B-2.*)
10. Just as Charles and Tibbit disappear, David returns to the library, just before he closes the door he turns to the imaginary occupant of the study and says:

stairs. Julie sits facing study, listening to David for all she is worth.)

CHARLES. (*To Tibbit, as they descend.*) . . . Now all this, exactly as it is. But *one* room. Just clean up the walls and the ceiling. (*Coming into the Library.*) And the new fittings for the kitchen will arrive next Tuesday. . . . (*Notices Julie by herself.*) Heh! What about the story?
JULIE. SSSH! We're doing it now.
CHARLES. (*Noticing odd noises in study.*) That's a hell of a way to write a story! What's he up to?
JULIE. Please! Go away. I'm trying to listen.

CHARLES. We're going to look at the cottages. I may be an hour or two. . . . (*Charles and Tibbit go onto terrace. Through the window we can see Charles demonstrating that the sundial is loose on its base. Tibbit makes a note and they disappear L.*)

*"So you just sit there—don't
move!"* Then he closes the door,
turns to Julie and says:

DAVID. (*To Julie.*) Well? What did you hear!

JULIE. Charles interrupted me so I couldn't make out what you were saying. It sounded as if you were talking to somebody.

DAVID. Good! Did you hear anything else?

JULIE. I don't think so. You slammed the door rather hard.

DAVID. (*Returns to study door.*) Harder than I need have perhaps. . . . (*He opens and slams door, but much more quietly.*) Now, the two women are in here; the two men in there . . . but you call Charles back in here—for some reason . . . (*He picks up tea cup from table and takes a sip.*)

JULIE. For what reason?

DAVID. Well? Why would you?

JULIE. (*Calling.*) Charles! Where's the Angostura bitters?

DAVID. Thank you. It's on the top shelf. (*Points to sideboard.*) But you say, "No it isn't, I've just looked."

JULIE. No it isn't, I've just looked.

DAVID. So Charles hunts around in here . . . and chats to you and the doctor . . . (*Pause. He crosses and leaves tea cup on sideboard.*) And then . . . when you've been talking for a minute or so . . . (*Another pause.*) . . . this may take a little longer than I meant it to . . . (*As he waits, he crosses* D. R. *He looks at his watch. Julie looks at David quite bewildered, then at her notes.*)

JULIE. There's just one thing—am I supposed to . . . ? (*In the study, the bang-contraption goes off with a loud bang and drops behind the chest. Julie gives a startled jump.*) Oh! I don't like this kind of murder story!

DAVID. It's all right. It won't do that again. Now I'm still Charles. He runs to this door. (*He rattles doorknob, then shouts.*) Open the door! . . . Are you all right? (*He throws his shoulder against door, pretending it is locked.*) Now you're the doctor. Come on, Doctor, this way.

JULIE. (*Protesting with a laugh.*) Heh! Where are we going? (*David snatches up Charles' overcoat from the chair and leads Julie through the library windows. They disappear* L. *and a few moments later enter by the study window, which is still open. David throws Charles' coat onto the floor to represent a body.*)

DAVID. Now that's the body. And while the doctor is pronouncing him well and truly dead . . . (*He goes to the study door.*) Charles pretends to unlock this door. (*He rattles key in door, then opens it.*)

JULIE. Which was never locked at all.

DAVID. And now—what else does the doctor see?

JULIE. (*Looking around.*) A well-burgled study!

DAVID. Go on then. What's been stolen?

JULIE. Whatever was in these drawers . . . the cigarette box . . . and . . . Oh! . . . the pistols!

DAVID. And how does the doctor know that?

JULIE. She just saw them when Charles was putting up that frame.

DAVID. (*Going to window.*) Good. Now you're the police. So what will *appear* to have happened?

JULIE. (*Going to the window.*) Well, the burglar must have come in through here . . . seen you. Pointed his gun at you . . . (*Crosses to study door.*) Then he heard us talking in there, so he locked this door.

DAVID. Yes, go on.

JULIE. Then he went through the desk, grabbed the cigarette box and those pistols. Then you made a move or started to shout and . . . bang! And then he ran out across the garden to his car and away. (*Going to David.*) Now show me the bang!

DAVID. Well, look around, you may see it. (*Julie looks around for a short moment and then says impatiently:*)

JULIE. Go on, show me! (*As David hauls up the bang-contraption from behind the chest. He is obviously very proud of this and demonstrates it as he describes it. NOTE: David should lift loop L off nail and take the bang-contraption over to Julie, so audience can see it more clearly.*)

DAVID. Here's your bang contraption. Just an old blank cartridge pistol of Clive's and two bits of string. . . . (*Julie puts her hands to her ears and closes her eyes.*) It's all right. It's not loaded now. (*Julie relaxes.*) You see, you use an ordinary cigarette as a fuse. So when it burns through this string—the pistol drops. This noose tightens round the trigger and—bang!

JULIE. Where's the cigarette?

DAVID. It falls behind that chest.

JULIE. And burns a hole in the carpet?

DAVID. (*Hanging gun back on the wall.*) Not if you've already sprayed it with soda water. (*Picks up wet cigarette from behind chest. Gives it to Julie.*) You see? One dead cigarette.

JULIE. Well, I'm sure that thing's all very ingenious but I don't understand it at all. You'll have to draw me a diagram or something.

DAVID. (*Laughs.*) I will. Anyway, it works.

JULIE. Yes, I heard it all right! (*She stares at chest for a moment, thoroughly perplexed, and then says:*) But I don't see how it kills you. (*As David collects grocery bag from outside window, takes out the silencer-pistol and crosses to desk.*)

DAVID. It doesn't. This is the gun that killed me.

JULIE. Is that a silencer?

DAVID. Yes. You see it still makes a noise. . . . But if when you fire it . . . (*Julie crosses to the study door and slams it as David pretends to fire the gun [i.e. the gun need not make any noise].*)

JULIE. I see! (*Snatching bag from David.*) What else have you got in this? (*As she takes out large shoes and drops them on desk with a laugh.*) Ah, the shoes!

DAVID. (*As he puts silencer-pistol on chest.*) Yes, Charles puts them on to make the footprints *before* I arrive with the doctor. . . . (*Julie points at bang-contraption.*)

JULIE. (*Interrupting.*) Yes I know, but what about that thing behind there? The police would find it the moment they arrive, wouldn't they?

DAVID. No they wouldn't, because the moment the doctor sees the body, Charles runs out after the burglar. Then you get the doctor back in there to phone the police. And as soon as Charles hears you talking on the phone . . . (*He goes out through the window and closes the curtains. A moment later we see his hand come through them and lift the bang-contraption off its nail behind the curtains. A moment later he re-enters and drops bang-contraption into the grocery bag.*)

JULIE. And into the bag of tricks! And where does *that* go? (*Points to bag.*) You can't leave it out there!

DAVID. No, Charles will have to hide it somewhere before the police arrive.

JULIE. Where? He won't have much time. (*David looks around the room for a moment.*)

DAVID. Well, there must be hundreds of places. (*He picks up the silencer-pistol from chest.*) Now, I'll show you once again . . .

JULIE. (*Excited.*) No, let *me* be Charles this time! (*She snatches*

26

the pistol from David, then picks up grocery bag.) Where does
this go?

DAVID. Behind the door. *(Julie hides bag behind door. David
pushes chest back against wall.)*

JULIE. So I bring you in here. . . . Go on! Turn around then!
(She laughs. He faces her.) And then . . . "pfft" says the
gun . . . ! *(She slams door with her other hand, then pauses,
confused.)* Then what?

DAVID. Just a second. I think you'll have to catch me as I fall
or I'll make too much noise. . . .

JULIE. *(She goes towards David.)* Wo'—Won't you be spurting
blood all over me?!

DAVID. Not if you hit me in the right place. I'll hardly bleed at
all. . . . Go on, run round and catch me! *(Julie does as told.
David starts to fall backwards and Julie catches him.)*

JULIE. Like that?

DAVID. Yes, that's it! Can you give me a sort of twist so I land
on my tummy? *(Julie tries to turn him, but he is too heavy and
falls to the floor. She also falls down.)* I'm so sorry. . . . My
fault. . . . *(They both rise.)* Let me show you. *(They change
positions.)* Now collapse completely. . . . *(Julie falls backwards,
he catches her.)* There! . . . And then round and down. . . . *(He
turns her around and lets her down to the floor.)* gently . . . like
that. . . . All right?

JULIE. *(Sitting on the floor and looking up at David, with a
smile.)* Yes, I'm fine. . . .

CURTAIN

ACT ONE

SCENE 3

*(The curtain should be down between Scenes 2 and 3
for as short a time as possible. This might be bridged by
the recorded sound of a grandfather clock striking the
three-quarter hour.)*

TIME: *Two hours later.*

ON RISE: *It is now dark outside. The library is dimly lit*

from the fire which is now burning. No other lights are on.
The library curtains are open, the study curtains are closed. The windows in both rooms are closed. The grocery bag is now on chair B.
Julie and David are sitting on the floor in front of the fire in the library. Their mood has changed completely. They seem to have forgotten all about their story. And the atmosphere is peaceful and romantic.

DAVID. . . . of course I tried very hard to forget Rodingham—I had to. And after all these years I thought I'd succeeded. Then when I heard about father I thought I'd just come and see him, once. I wasn't even planning to stay the night. (*Pause.*) Did you ever go back to your home?

JULIE. Not after we sold it. I don't think I could have done.

DAVID. Just as well. As soon as I turned into the drive I felt as though I'd never been away. It may look a mess but it really hasn't changed at all—not for me. Of course when father . . . threw me out—I made all sorts of plans to get back here. (*Laughs.*) I knew Clive would go broke one day and then I'd come back and buy the whole place from him. But things never quite work out, do they?

JULIE. Not as you plan them. When we sold our home, I gave myself two years to get just one story published. After five years I ended up as one of Charles' secretaries. . . . Let's finish the story shall we?

DAVID. I'd love to show you our village sometime, perhaps we could . . . but I was forgetting—Charles knows it as well as I do, or better. I'm sorry.

JULIE. No, as a matter of fact he—we'd be very grateful if you would. And what's that other village we came through today? Where I got stuck?

DAVID. The Duke's village?

JULIE. Oh yes that's right. . . . Do you know the Duke?

DAVID. Uncle Graham! We're not actually related but he's Clive's godfather. You may find him a bit fierce to begin with but I'm sure he'll like you. . . . (*Sound of Charles' car approaching and headlights on the window.*)

JULIE. David. The story.

28

DAVID. What story?

JULIE. (*Rising.*) It's all very well for you. I've got to write it. (*As David gets up slowly and switches on lights, Julie peers into grocery bag.*) Now! Where on earth are they going to hide this? So far they've got four pistols—a large pair of shoes—cigarette box. . . . They might as well sign their confessions and pop them in as well. (*During Julie's above speech we see Charles and Tibbit appear outside library window. They have a last few words. Then Tibbit disappears L. As Charles enters by library window:*) Charles, where would you hide something around here?

CHARLES. What is it, a body? (*On this thought, David runs into study, picks up Charles' overcoat from floor and dusts it off.*)

JULIE. No, only this. (*Holds up bag.*) But it's frightfully incriminating.

CHARLES. You've got four hundred acres. Bury it. Well? Did you make any progress?

JULIE. He's given me a marvelous idea. (*She puts grocery bag back on chair B.*)

CHARLES. (*In whisper.*) But what about the *Duke?* (*David now re-enters the library with Charles' coat.*)

JULIE. Mr. Rodingham very kindly suggested showing me around the village next week.

CHARLES. (*Loudly.*) Good idea! Make it Tuesday. I'll be here supervising the new kitchen. Just wait till you see that! Stainless steel from floor to ceiling! (*He puts a possessive arm around Julie's shoulders.*)

DAVID. (*Holds out Charles' coat.*) I'll expect you on Tuesday, then. (*As David helps Charles on with his coat:*)

CHARLES. By the way, that sundial. Your brother said it was a present from Charles the First. Was he pulling my leg?

DAVID. The Second, actually. He was always staying here.

CHARLES. Was he? Well anyway, it needs fixing. You can twist it around like a steering wheel. (*As David helps Julie on with her coat:*)

DAVID. Yes, my father liked to set his watch by it and he would keep adjusting it for daylight saving time. (*They laugh.*) I'll fix it before you move in.

CHARLES. (*As he opens French windows.*) Just a dab of builder's cement underneath and then set it by the sun when it's on the hour. . . .

JULIE. (*Excited, pointing at grocery bag.*) The bag of tricks!

DAVID. What?

JULIE. He could hide it in a hole underneath the sundial! (*Julie goes out to sundial and looks back towards the telephone.*) And look! As it's dark, he could watch the doctor and me phoning the police at the same time, without being seen himself . . . ! (*Charles joins Julie on terrace.*)

CHARLES. Now that's enough of that! You can tell me your whole story on the way home.

DAVID. (*As he joins them at window.*) Don't you dare! Never tell anyone a story before it's written. You lose half your steam.

CHARLES. (*With a laugh.*) All right then, I'll read it in the Evening News, eh? And in the meantime not a word to anyone else, either. (*He exits L.*)

DAVID. Not a word. (*The phone starts to ring.*) Excuse me.

JULIE. Goodbye and thank you so much. (*Julie and David shake hands and she exits L. David calls after them with a laugh.*)

DAVID. Don't tell him now! (*The moment they have gone, his laugh dies. He stares back at the sundial for a moment or two, checking as to whether he could be seen from the telephone. Then he crosses to table, picks up phone and as he talks he reaches over to chair B for the grocery bag and puts it on writing table.*) Hello? . . . Oh, hello, Liz. . . . You just missed the Sturrocks. . . . (*As he continues, he takes the various articles from the grocery bag and lays them carefully on the table, one by one. His entire concentration is on these objects, as he talks on absent-mindedly as though hardly realizing what he is saying.*) Yes . . . they're moving in here in about three weeks. . . . Hmmmm? . . . Yes—I rather like old Charles. He's all right! . . . (*Finally, as he takes out the silencer-pistol and stares at it in his hand.*) I think they might get along here . . . rather well . . . !

CURTAIN

AUDIO BRIDGE

(*Recorded Between Scenes 3 and 4 of Act I.*)

(*Phone rings.*)

JULIE. Hullo.

DAVID. Hullo, Julie.

JULIE. Oh, hullo, David. I'd meant to phone you and thank you for showing me around the village. . . . It was a *lovely* day.

DAVID. Yes, it was. Could I have a quick word with Charles? It's about . . .

JULIE. He should be home any minute.

DAVID. I was wondering if . . .

JULIE. I posted you the copy of my story the day before yesterday. . . .

DAVID. Got it this morning. And very well done.

JULIE. Unless you can think of anything else, I might as well enter it right away—don't you think? (*Slight pause.*)

DAVID. Er—I did notice a couple of snags. . . . *When* does it have to be in?

JULIE. Friday week. Can you give me them now? (*Slight pause.*)

DAVID. It's a bit difficult on the phone. If you'd like to come down here again tomorrow . . .

JULIE. I don't think we *can* come down again. Not before we move in.

DAVID. Oh—well . . . I could come up to London if that's any good.

JULIE. I don't think so. You see—well, Charles hasn't been too well this last week.

DAVID. Oh, I'm sorry. (*Sound starts fading.*)

JULIE. It's nothing very much, but . . . anyway, we'll be moving in a week from Wednesday. . . .

(*Curtain rises on Scene 4.*)

ACT ONE

SCENE 4

TIME: *Three weeks later. Night.*

ALTERATIONS TO SET: *The footstool is in front of chair A. Chair B has been moved to R. of writing table and faces front. On chair C is David's duffle coat and knapsack. The rear wheel of his bicycle can be seen outside against left of window.*

ON RISE: *David is looking out of window. The fire is burning. Otherwise the stage is dark. The curtains in both*

31

rooms are open. Dark outside. Then, headlights on window and sound of car. David quickly picks up the copy of Julie's story from the table, looks around for a moment and then places it very deliberately on chair A. He then goes quickly upstairs as Charles and Julie pass the library window. Charles carries a large suitcase, an attache case and his briefcase, Julie a small suitcase and portable typewriter. A moment later they enter from hall leaving luggage in doorway. Charles switches on library lights. As they enter:

JULIE. . . . he's probably gone to bed by now.

CHARLES. He's not staying here *tonight?*

JULIE. I expect so. Why not?

CHARLES. Our first night in Rodingham? (*David comes downstairs.*)

DAVID. (*Cheerfully.*) Ah! Welcome!

JULIE. Oh, hello David. I hope you didn't wait up specially. You're staying tonight, of course?

DAVID. (*He goes to fireplace.*) No. Dr. Woolley's invited me over the weekend. So—it's all yours!

JULIE. We'll drive you to the Doctor's then.

DAVID. It's all right, thanks. Got my bike outside. (*During the above Charles takes his attache case and briefcase to the writing table. He looks tired and out of sorts and his attitude to David is now clearly hostile.*)

CHARLES. Where's the rest of our luggage?

DAVID. I had it put in the bedroom. Was that all right?

CHARLES. (*As he crosses to hall and goes upstairs with his suitcase.*) Well, we mustn't keep you up any longer, Mr. Rodingham.

DAVID. If you need anything you'll let me . . .

CHARLES. (*Curtly.*) That's right. *Goodnight.* (*Disappears upstairs.*)

JULIE. (*As though to apologize.*) Thank you for waiting up. And having everything ready.

DAVID. A Mrs. Clegg from the village will come every morning at nine till you find someone else.

JULIE. Thank you so much.

DAVID. (*Pause.*) So, I'll say goodnight. (*For a moment he looks sadly around the room, playing on her emotions.*) I do hope you'll be very happy here. (*He picks up coat and knapsack from chair C.*)

JULIE. And I hope you'll come and see us, very often . . . Oh, Dr. Woolley is coming here for supper tomorrow. You'll come as well, of course.

DAVID. (*With a glance upstairs.*) Thanks, but I don't think I should.

JULIE. Charles is still a bit out of sorts tonight, but don't let that worry you.

DAVID. (*Quietly.*) I won't. (*Pause. He glances at the story on the chair, but Julie still does not notice it.*) Well, goodnight. (*Crosses to library window. As he goes out he turns and calls back.*) Oh, and good luck with the story. (*Exits, closing window, wheels bicycle off L.*)

JULIE. Oh the story! I nearly forgot! (*She opens window.*) Have you just a minute?

DAVID. (*Appearing in open window.*) But haven't you—sent it in yet?

JULIE. (*Surprised.*) No. You told me not to. . . . You said there were a couple of things . . . (*He comes back into room, closes window. He has left coat and knapsack on bicycle which is now out of sight.*)

DAVID. (*Vaguely.*) Oh yes, there was something. . . . Now where did I leave my copy . . . ? (*He pretends to search for it on writing table. Julie sees it on chair A and hands it to him*).

JULIE. Here it is. Let me get mine.

DAVID. How many copies did you make?

JULIE. Just these two. (*As they talk she carries her typewriter from hall to chair B, zips open its case and takes out her copy of the story from an addressed envelope all ready for posting.*)

DAVID. (*Turning pages.*) Can't remember what it was now. (*Pause.*) Did Charles like it?

JULIE. Oh he hasn't been allowed to read it yet. I *must* post it tomorrow at the latest. Now what was it?

DAVID. Bottom of page twelve. Why doesn't he cement up the sundial as we said?

JULIE. (*Referring to her copy.*) He just wouldn't have time. It would only take a few seconds to phone the police. . . .

DAVID. That's all he needs. Look. (*He demonstrates using chair B as though it was the sundial. Julie keeps glancing from chair to*

33

sundial outside.) He has already dug his hole underneath and makes a little bed of cement around the edge. Now it takes several hours for cement to set, so he need only tip it back on one edge, shove in the grocery bag and let it down again. And by morning it will be set as hard as a rock. . . . (*During the end of David's speech, Charles comes down the stairs.*)

CHARLES. (*From portal.*) *Still* here, Mr. Rodingham?

DAVID. Yes. We just had another idea on the story.

CHARLES. (*To Julie, as he crosses to writing table. As they talk, he sits at table, takes check book from briefcase and writes check.*) You said it was finished.

JULIE. It is, but there's still time to . . .

CHARLES. You can't go on rewriting it forever.

DAVID. It doesn't need to be in 'til the day after tomorrow. . . .

CHARLES. Then he can post it tonight. Take all that trouble and then get it in too late! (*Writing check.*) But before you go, Mr. Rodingham . . . I always meant to give you something . . . when you *left* us. . . . (*While Charles is writing check, Julie hands her copy of the story in its envelope to David and he drops his copy onto side table.*) There! (*Charles puts check down on writing table. After a pause David crosses to table and picks it up.*)

DAVID. (*Bewildered.*) Is this for my brother?

CHARLES. No. It's made out to you, isn't it. . . . I said you wouldn't be out of pocket.

DAVID. Then you've made a mistake. You've written one thousand pounds! (*David lays check down on side table.*)

CHARLES. Well, I don't think that's unreasonable. Particularly . . .

JULIE. Charles!

CHARLES. (*Louder.*) Particularly as you're not likely to be working together again. I mean you understand, don't you? Mrs. Sturrock doesn't want *all* her stories written for her. . . .

DAVID. I didn't write any of this . . .

CHARLES. And as you're leaving Rodingham. That's right, isn't it? You're not planning to hang around here, are you?

DAVID. No, I'm not, but . . .

CHARLES. So there you are. It's one thing to do something for a friend who you're going to see again—and again. But that's not exactly the case, is it?

DAVID. I don't know *what* you're talking about. . . .

34

CHARLES. (*Rises and moves to fireplace.*) I think you understand very well, Mr. Rodingham. As far as I'm concerned it's a fair deal all round.

JULIE. Goodnight, David.

DAVID. (*To Julie, quietly.*) Goodnight . . . I'll see you tomorrow evening then.

CHARLES. When?

DAVID. Isn't Dr. Woolley coming here . . . tomorrow?

CHARLES. *She* is, yes. I'm picking her up on my way back from London.

DAVID. Well I'm staying with her, you see. I think she'll expect me to come as well. . . . If I didn't, I'd hardly know how to explain it to her . . . would you? (*Pause. Charles appears at a loss and turns to fire.*)

JULIE. Well *certainly* you must come.

CHARLES. (*Sulkily.*) If this is going to turn into a dinner party, you'll need some help from the village.

JULIE. No, I'll manage.

DAVID. (*To Julie.*) I'll come a little early and give you a hand —and I can fix that *sundial* at the same time.

CHARLES. (*Points to study wall.*) The builders are taking out that wall on Monday. They can do it then. (*A pause. David glances round at study wall for a moment.*)

DAVID. No, they'll only mess it up. And I know exactly how to do it. (*To Julie.*) I'd better come about two then.

CHARLES. Why so early?

DAVID. Well, I'll need the sun, you see . . . before it disappears behind the house. (*David holds out the story-envelope to Julie, inviting her to take it.*) Then I think you *should* retype those few pages . . . ?

CHARLES. (*Angrily.*) You'll post it *as it is!* Tonight! (*Pause. David looks straight at Charles, then very quietly.*)

DAVID. As you wish. (*He turns to exit, with the envelope.*)

CHARLES. Haven't you forgotten something, Mr. Rodingham? (*David turns. After a long pause he goes quietly to the writing table, picks up the check, exits by library window, and disappears* L., *taking story-envelope with him.*) Exit the Rodinghams! (*After a moment Julie picks up typewriter from chair B and takes it into study. Charles goes to writing table.*)

JULIE. I just hope you'll apologize tomorrow night.

CHARLES. (*Amused.*) I will not. (*Takes red file out of briefcase, drops it on table.*) And fancy inviting himself to dinner like that. How thick-skinned can you get? (*Opens attache case and unpacks three books.*) You mustn't grudge me that little gesture. I've been itching to send the Rodinghams packing for thirty years.

JULIE. (*From study.*) What has he ever done to you?

CHARLES. Well, now you mention it, he should have had more sense than to take you round the village like that. Introducing you to every tradesman as if you were his latest girl friend. (*Takes a small whiskey bottle from attache case.*)

JULIE. (*Returning to the library. She partly closes the study door.*) But you asked him to introduce me. . . .

CHARLES. Not to the blacksmith and the green grocer. I just wanted you to meet his Uncle Graham and his Aunt Edie. (*Takes a small whiskey bottle from attache case.*)

JULIE. (*Crossing to the R. of Charles.*) Charles . . . I think we'll have to take our time getting to know these people. This is one time you can't just barge in and . . .

CHARLES. Now don't you give me "can't." I'll soon learn their lingo. Got it all here . . . (*As he picks up his three books and drops them on the table one by one.*) . . . Who's Who . . . All About Horses . . . All About Dogs. . . . I'll mug this up in a month—you'll see! (*He takes his whiskey bottle to the sideboard. He gets a glass and pours whiskey into it.*) So—the Duke was nice to you, was he?

JULIE. Yes, he was very charming.

CHARLES. And so he should be with a nine-hole golf course of his own. And a castle in Scotland! To which he may be retiring sooner than he thinks. (*Takes a drink.*) Julie, now we're here you might as well learn a few secrets too. (*A pause.*) Do you really think I intend to live in this *barracks?*

JULIE. What do you mean?

CHARLES. It wasn't this house I wanted from Master Clive. It was his land. Four hundred acres. Now worth a few hundred each. In a few years, ten, twenty times as much. There've been whispers of building a new motorway from London to the coast. So far it's barely a rumour, but if they do it will bring us within an hour of London. In ten years we could be a booming suburb. Stage one was to get our foot in the door. And so here we are! (*He sits in chair A, very much the Lord of the Manor.*)

JULIE. Why didn't you tell me this?

CHARLES. I thought I'd make your work a little easier. That's all. I wanted young Rodingham to introduce you to the local gentry. Because stage two is for us to become one of *them*. We're going to play Lord and Lady of the manor. Champions of the English countryside. Strictly anti-progress. And why? Because they're a very conservative bunch around here and they don't like greedy businessmen who try to gobble up their land. So they'll never sell to the speculators when they begin to nibble. But they'll sell to *me*—and laugh down their sleeves—because I'm poor old Charlie Sturrock the grocery boy who's now trying to be a big landlord! Bring me the red file on the table there. . . . (*Julie goes to writing table.*) And while they're having a good laugh I'll buy up every acre I can get my hands on. (*She brings him the red file and turns to the fire. He takes from it a map and spreads it on the footstool in front of his chair. He beckons to her and she moves to R. of chair A. He talks excitedly like a boy with a new toy.*) Julie—here. Now this is my blueprint. This is all ours. And here's the Duke's estate. Now he'll be the main opposition, so sooner or later, I'll buy this Longmeadow Farm and get a squeeze on him. Then I can ring his golf course with nasty little houses and send him north. Stage three: we'll bring in some quick middle class money. Here . . . and here. Two acre plots for the stock brokers and company directors. And then when the whole place is booming and ever so classy—stage four: we let in the riff raff, little quarter-acre plots, thousands of 'em, all jammed up together with our own bus line to race 'em in and out of London. And we'll get a percentage of all the pickings, the laundries and the supermarkets. Oh, Julie! We'll make a killing!

JULIE. (*Turns to fireplace.*) And I really thought you were going to retire this time.

CHARLES. (*Folds map and laughs.*) To the feudal village of Rodingham? I'll never know which I despise more—the place or the people.

JULIE. But we are going to live here?

CHARLES. (*Puts map in red file. Rises, leaves glass on table, and crosses to the writing table, where he puts the file in the briefcase and the briefcase into drawer of table.* NOTE: *The writing table has one [or two] drawers at the top. These drawers must be on* the *downstage side. See also Act II, Scene 2.*) Until stage three, we'll just use these few rooms—like a flat. Then I have plans to turn the whole house into a country club, so the two-acre boys can dine every weekend in (*Mimicking.*) "Lord Rodingham's old place." This room will be the bar. The ballroom will take thirty small tables. That's why I needed the *new kitchen* and the *wine cellar!* (*He crosses to the sideboard for his bottle.*)

JULIE. And where do we live in stage four?

CHARLES. What's wrong with the way we've been living? (*Brings bottle to* L. *of round table.*)

JULIE. (*Crossing to the footstool, sits.*) You mean—different hotels. . . .

CHARLES. But better ones. And we're going to travel. Rome and Paris and the South of France. (*Puts glass on table, sits down and leans over to Julie.*) We're going to have some good times, Julie. (*Takes her in his arms.*) We'll dress you up. . . .

JULIE. (*Rises, goes to the fireplace.*) Charles, I—I don't think I can go on living in hotels.

CHARLES. What's wrong with them? It saves *you* a lot of trouble.

JULIE. I just can't write when we're . . .

CHARLES. Ah! The writing . . . yes, that's important. Well now . . . there must be some solution. I tell you what. (*Rises. Crosses* L. *a few steps.*) How would you like . . . a little flat of your own . . . in London? Where you could be completely alone? (*As they talk in library, David enters the study by the French window. The story is in his coat pocket. The study door is slightly open and he pauses to listen.*)

JULIE. That might help a lot. You see, there are times when I'm writing that I just have to be . . .

CHARLES. Completely alone?

JULIE. That's right. Just until I've thought the story out . . .

CHARLES. (*Interrupting.*) And then—if you should get a little tired of being *completely* alone—you could always invite your little writing friends . . .

JULIE. No, I . . .

CHARLES. Like David Rodingham?

JULIE. (*Angrily.*) No, I did not mean that. (*Charles laughs. He is now beginning to enjoy himself. He pours another drink and as he talks he moves around the room. He switches out the sideboard lamp and wall brackets [same switch]. Then he goes into the study. David moves behind the door. Charles locks study window and draws curtains shut, then returns to library, leaving door open. He talks all the time. Julie sits quite still and stares hopelessly at the fire.)*

CHARLES. *(Laughs.)* I suppose most wives have some pet excuse for doing what they like now and then. So with you it's your writing! That day he showed you around the village . . . that's when it started. But he let you down a bit tonight, didn't he? I never thought he'd take money like that, not in front of you. He almost reminded me of that nice Mr. Hopkins in the Accounts Department, who used to hang around you before we were married. Now I only gave him five hundred pounds, and you never saw *him* again, did you?

JULIE. *(Quietly.)* Why did you marry me?

CHARLES. *(Casually, as he locks library windows and draws curtains closed.)* Because you were a lady. And I didn't have too much choice. Does that answer your question? *(He crosses to writing table and turns out the lamp leaving only the fire light. He goes to the round table, picks up the bottle of whiskey. Julie shows no sign of moving.)* Now don't hang around down here all night. This is an occasion! And we have the whole house to ourselves! . . . I wonder if the Rodingham ghosts are out tonight! *(Singing as he goes to the hall and upstairs.)* Oh little Lord David, how do you do? Where's Clive? Yoo-hoo! Where's Clive? Yoo-hoo! *(He disappears upstairs. Julie sits frozen and frightened. David comes from behind the door and into the library, while the clock in the hall strikes the quarter hour, David crosses R., takes Charles' check from his pocket. Julie turns, sees him, and rises, startled. Then he crumples it up, crosses to the fireplace and tosses it into the fire. Suddenly Julie runs to him and buries herself in his arms. Finally, David pushes her away gently and looks her straight in the eyes until she is calm. Then he lifts the story-envelope from his pocket and holds it out to her. But Julie only stares at the envelope as though frightened to touch it. David tears it in half, steps over to the fire and drops it in. He waits until it lights up, then turns, takes her by the hands and says, quietly:)*

DAVID. Tomorrow. *(Then he leaves her and crosses to the study window. Julie runs after him and calls in a whisper:)*

JULIE. David! *(But he ignores her and lets himself out. When he has disappeared, she turns back to the fire and stares at it, horrified at its implication. Then she sees the other copy of the story, which still lies on the side table. Julie moves towards it, picks it up, but after a moment she drops it back on table and turns away. Then Charles calls harshly from upstairs:)*

CHARLES. *(Off.)* Ju . . . lie! Don't hang around down there all night! *(Very slowly she picks up the story, drops it into the fire and as it blazes up, turns and goes up the stairs.)*

CURTAIN

ACT TWO

Scene 1

TIME: *The following evening.*

ALTERATIONS TO SET: *The library is fully lit but the study is lit only by the desk lamp. The curtains in the study are closed. The curtains in the library are open a little (so that David can see the car lights to warn him). It is dark outside. The study door is wide open. The desk chair has been placed under the pistol frames. On the desk is a hammer. In the library the footstool is placed above the fireplace. The bang-contraption is in position B-1, out of sight behind chest.*

ON RISE: *David is in the study, waiting. He is holding the battle axe which has been taken off the wall. He looks at his watch impatiently. Julie comes halfway down the stairs and calls from the portal, but David doesn't hear her.*

Both Julie and David are tense and nervous and speak quietly.

JULIE. David! (*She goes to the study door and sees David.*) It's over half an hour! Hadn't you better try phoning the doctor again?

DAVID. I did. There's no answer. They must be on their way by now.

JULIE. (*Notices the axe in David's hand.*) What's that for?

DAVID. When they first come in here, I shall be fixing this back on the wall. Then the doctor can't help noticing the pistols. (*He leans axe against chest and enters library. Julie follows.*)

JULIE. Have you made the footprints?

DAVID. I've done everything. There's nothing to do now, but wait. You'd better go upstairs. (*She crosses to stairs, then turns.*)

41

JULIE. (*Nervous and frightened.*) David, I still don't know *exactly* when you want me to come down.

DAVID. (*Impatiently.*) When the doctor has been in there and seen the pistols, I'll bring her back in here. We've been over this . . .

JULIE. (*Impatiently.*) Yes! But how will *I* know?

DAVID. (*Glancing at study, trying to visualize and time it.*) Wait exactly one minute after you hear the front door slam. Got a watch? . . . Here, take this. (*He takes off his wristwatch and gives it to her. She clutches it tightly in her hand as they talk.*) Go up then and don't worry. We've thought of everything.

JULIE. But we *haven't!* What happens *afterwards?* We haven't thought of that at all! When it's . . . all over . . . what should I do then?

DAVID. Nothing. Just leave everything to me.

JULIE. No! I don't mean that! Shouldn't I . . . faint or something?

DAVID. (*A pause. Then very seriously.*) Have you ever fainted before?

JULIE. (*As though ashamed.*) No, I haven't.

DAVID. Then don't! If you did it wrong, the doctor would get suspicious immediately. . . .

JULIE. But I'll have to do *something!*

DAVID. Then make it a delayed reaction. Behave almost as if nothing has happened and then . . . break up a bit, later on.

JULIE. (*Weakly.*) David, it's not too late to change our minds . . .

DAVID. (*Impatiently.*) Look, they can't be long now!

JULIE. (*Strongly.*) I can't do it!

DAVID. You aren't going to do anything!

JULIE. I can't let you do it! (*Sound of car and headlights on window. He makes a dive for window and closes curtains.*)

DAVID. Here they come. Quickly!

JULIE. (*Frantically.*) No! I'll leave him tonight. I wouldn't mind where or how we lived . . . would you?

DAVID. (*Violently.*) It would be no good. You must know that by now. (*Sound of car door slamming.*)

JULIE. David I—I just can't do it! (*She turns and runs up the stairs. He stands quite still and watches her until she reaches the portal. Then, with great tenseness but quietly.*)

42

DAVID. This is our only chance. (*For a moment, she turns, then she continues and disappears upstairs. He shouts after her.*) I'm going to do it! (*David goes into study, picks up the hammer, climbs on chair and taps wall. Dr. Woolley [unseen] passes window and then front doorbell rings. David waits a moment, undecided whether to answer it or not. Bell rings again. David puts down hammer, crosses library and opens front door. Cheerfully.*) Hello, Liz! What's been keeping you? . . . I thought Charles was going to pick you up. . . . (*He slams the front door shut.*)

WOOLLEY. (*Coming straight into library. She puts her doctor's bag down on stool.*) Where's Mrs. Sturrock?

DAVID. (*Casually.*) I think she's upstairs or in the kitchen. (*Trying to lead Woolley into Study.*) Do you mind coming in here one second? I was just trying to fix something onto the . . .

WOOLLEY. Charlie's had an accident . . . (*David turns.*) He was on his way to pick me up in his car.

DAVID. (*After a pause.*) Yes. . . . Is it—bad?

WOOLLEY. (*Simply.*) I'm afraid he's dead. (*Pause.*) He hit a truck, head on, in that new one-way street by Wollock's Groceries. As a boy, he must have shot around that same corner a thousand times on his bicycle. Where is she?

DAVID. I . . . let me tell her. (*He moves toward stairs but Woolley stops him.*)

WOOLLEY. No. I'd be better at that, David. You see, we have to try and make her think of it first.

DAVID. All right, I won't tell her, but just let me bring her down here. (*Julie starts to come down the stairs.*)

WOOLLEY. Well, I'll go up with you . . .

DAVID. No, wait, Liz!

JULIE. (*Descending.*) Good evening, Doctor. Did either of you notice anyone outside just now? I thought I saw a big . . .

DAVID. (*Overlapping, to try and stop her.*) Julie! (*But she brushes past David and crosses towards study.*)

JULIE. (*Looking around.*) Where's Charles?

WOOLLEY. (*Firmly, but very kind.*) Mrs. Sturrock. I have very bad news . . . so you've got to be brave . . .

JULIE. (*Standing dead still.*) Yes? (*Woolley speaks gently but slowly as if to drive it home.*)

WOOLLEY. Charles has had an accident . . . in the village. . . .

A bad one. (*Julie stares back at her. She seems a hundred miles away and has forgotten everything else.*)

JULIE. Then I'll go to him at once. (*She starts to go, Woolley stops her.*)

WOOLLEY. I'm afraid there's nothing you can do now. (*Pause.*) Come and sit down.

JULIE. (*Angrily.*) But I *must* go to him! Where is he?

DAVID. (*Almost harshly to force her attention.*) Julie! (*Then quieter.*) He's dead. (*Behind Woolley's back he raises his hand to warn her. Julie stares at David as if she has never seen him before.*)

WOOLLEY. (*Gently.*) He was in his car. It was quite instantaneous. I'd better take you to my house tonight, but perhaps you'd like to rest a little first. . . .

JULIE. (*Calmly.*) I'll be all right. I think I'll just stay here for a bit.

DAVID. I'll bring her along.

WOOLLEY. I'll give you something that will help you to relax. (*As Woolley crosses to her bag, on stool, and opens it:*)

JULIE. No, I'd rather you went now . . . if you don't mind. . . . (*She holds on to chair B to steady herself and then as she slowly collapses onto the floor in a faint:*) I'm perfectly . . . all right . . . (*As she hits the floor David rushes towards her.*)

DAVID. Julie! You don't have to . . . ! (*Then, as Woolley turns and David pulls up sharply and stares down at Julie . . .*)

QUICK CURTAIN

AUDIO BRIDGE

(*Between Scenes 1 and 2 in Act II*)

(*Phone rings several times. Woolley picks it up.*)

WOOLLEY. (*Sleepy.*) Hello. . . .

DAVID. Liz! David. Hope I didn't wake you.

WOOLLEY. You did.

DAVID. Oh, I'm terribly sorry.

WOOLLEY. (*Furious.*) Do you realize what time it is? Not a word from you for nearly a year and then you wake me up in the middle of the *night!*

DAVID. It's only ten o'clock. And I have *big* news!

WOOLEY. What is it?

DAVID. I'm married!

WOOLLEY. Well, that's no excuse! . . . Who is she?

DAVID. Oh, just someone I knew once. Ran into her quite recently in Selfridges of all places. Fell like a ton of bricks!

WOOLLEY. Well, bring her round in the morning and I'll tell you what *I* think. *Goodnight*, David.

DAVID. Goodnight Liz.

WOOLLEY. And give my love to *Julie*.

DAVID. Yes, I will. . . . Heh! How the hell did you know?!

WOOLLEY. I haven't been a doctor for forty years for nothing! Never expected anything else. When did *you* finally get round to it?

DAVID. About three weeks ago. We honeymooned on my houseboat and now we're driving around staying at pubs and house hunting.

WOOLLEY. What's the mater with Rodingham?

DAVID. Well, Julie thinks it's too big. She's had it closed for months, but we're on our way there now—just for the night. (*Start fading.*) If the phone's working, I'll call you in the morning. . .

(*Curtain rises on Act II, Scene 2*)

ACT TWO

SCENE 2

TIME: *About a year later. Night.*

ALTERATIONS TO SET: *The house has been empty for several months. Curtains in the study are closed. The library curtains are open but shutters cover these windows from outside. The library furniture has been covered with dust sheets. A pile of mail, magazines, etc., lies on the floor inside the front door. Chair D has been moved D. R. and faces L.*

NOTE: *The shutters and dust sheets are for atmosphere*

only and if they should unduly prolong the interval between the scenes they could be omitted.

Both rooms are dark. (*There is moonlight outside.*) After a few moments we hear footsteps on the terrace and Julie and David enter by the front door, treading on the mail as they come in. They both wear raincoats, which they keep on throughout this scene.

JULIE. (*As they enter.*) Can't see a thing!

DAVID. Mind the step. (*He lights his cigarette lighter and picks up the mail. Julie enters library and tries the light switch.*)

JULIE. The electricity's off.

DAVID. (*Enters library with mail.*) Quite a pile of mail here. You check the telephone and I'll find some candles. (*He exits to the kitchen. Julie crosses to writing table and removes dust sheets. She puts mail on table and picks up the phone, rattles the receiver and then hangs up. Then she turns suddenly and looks upstairs, frightened. David enters from kitchen with candelabra, [one candle lighted] crosses and puts it on writing table. As he crosses:*)

JULIE. David!

DAVID. What's the matter?

JULIE. I . . . I heard something upstairs. (*David listens for several seconds.*)

DAVID. (*Lightly.*) No, that's just a creak. This house creaks all over. I know every one of them. (*He hands her the mail and lights the other candles.*) Let's see what we've got here. (*Julie whisks through it, hands David a letter. She sits in chair C above table.*)

JULIE. This is probably that list of securities we asked for.

DAVID. Oh, thanks.. (*As he opens it and glances through it.*) No letters for me, I suppose?

JULIE. Don't think so . . . a few for Clive. (*David pockets list of securities.*)

DAVID. I'll send them to his bank manager. He *always* knows where he is. (*He sits in chair B facing R. side of writing table.*)

JULIE. Let's sort all this stuff later. Put it in something and then to bed. I'm freezing. (*She rises. As they talk David searches in the drawer of the writing table for something to put the mail in. He finds Charles' briefcase and empties its contents onto the table and hands it to Julie. One of the things that came out of the briefcase was Charles' red file.*)

46

DAVID. Still no offers to buy Rodingham?

JULIE. (*Putting the mail in the briefcase.*) I don't think so. (*David picks up the red file and glances through it casually.*)

DAVID. Darling, when we *do* find this small convenient place you're looking for . . .

JULIE. Yes?

DAVID. Then what? (*She stands behind him and puts her arms around him.*)

JULIE. Start working again, of course. I want to write that story we thought up on the houseboat.

DAVID. Well, good. We'll write it together. Trouble is—they're so damned expensive, aren't they?

JULIE. What's expensive?

DAVID. Small convenient houses. Now if you'd only spend the same amount on this place, we'd soon have it back in shape.

JULIE. (*Moving away from him.*) We are *never* going to live here, David. (*Pause.*)

DAVID. And *why* not? (*Pause. Then slowly.*) There is only one reason, isn't there? Because you can't face . . .

JULIE. (*Quickly, interrupting.*) Because we can't afford it. You wouldn't stop with the house. You'd want to fix up the cottages and then the village. In ten years all this would have been spent and we'd be back where your father was. (*During her above speech David has picked up the red file again and is reading it more intently.*)

DAVID. Darling, these papers were in that briefcase. Shouldn't they have gone to your solicitors?

JULIE. No . . . that's all finished with. (*She takes him by the hand and tries to pull him away from the table but he holds fast, still looking at file.*)

DAVID. Heh! Where are you going? Wait a minute. (*Turns page.*) What is all this?

JULIE. It was just a project for developing the neighborhood. Come on, let's leave this till tomorrow.

DAVID. Why on earth didn't you tell me about this?

JULIE. (*Strongly.*) Because it has *nothing* to do with *us*.

DAVID. (*Still whisking through file.*) A motorway from London! If this is so, it will send the price of land sky high! Perhaps we should be buying, not selling! That's it. . . . Keep Rodingham, forget the repairs and use these investments of yours to buy up all the land we can get and then sit back and wait for the price to go up . . . !

JULIE. (*Moving to stairs.*) Do we have to talk about this tonight?

DAVID. (*Lightly.*) No harm in discussing it, is there?

JULIE. (*Moving* D. R.) Well, I don't want to. And I don't want to live here. And to hear you go on about *buying* this and *buying* that, anyone would think you were . . . (*Long pause.*)

DAVID. (*Very quietly.*) Anyone would think I was . . . Charles?

JULIE. No! I didn't mean that. I'm sorry, but I did tell you not to bring me here tonight. (*As David throws red file on table, rises and crosses to Julie, who is standing* D. R.)

DAVID. (*Gently.*) It's all right, darling. I've said it now. (*Slowly and deliberately.*) Charles. Charles. Charles. That's the one word we've managed to avoid all this time. That's the *only* reason you won't live here, isn't it?

JULIE. I didn't want to bring this up—especially tonight.

DAVID. (*Putting his arm 'round her.*) I'm glad. We should have done it before, that's all. Perhaps I should have started off each day by saying . . . (*Very quickly and cheerfully.*) Good morning, Darling! Well, here we are! And just to think that less than a year ago we were planning to murder your husband Charles. But fortunately he was killed in an accident—now what's for breakfast? (*Julie breaks away from him and crosses below writing table.*) The whole point is—it never happened!

JULIE. (*Turning.*) But we were *going* to do it!

DAVID. But so many things could have stopped it. The phone might have rung at just the wrong moment. Liz Woolley might have had to leave suddenly and so I could never have done it anyway. You see, that's the one solid fact I've hung on to all this time, *I might never have done it!*

JULIE. (*Wearily.*) You work this out as best you can. I'll have to do it my way. (*She turns to stairs, but he holds her attention.*)

DAVID. Getting away from here won't help. There's only one way to close this door now. Stay here and fight it out. Write that new story of yours. And you know where you should do that . . . (*He takes the candles and leads the way to the dark study.*) In here . . . (*She holds back.*) Come on. I'll help you. (*She follows him slowly into study.*) Let's talk about it now. (*He puts the candelabra on the study desk.*) Spoilt city girl falls in love with artist and tries to live on his houseboat. Is that right?

JULIE. Yes. I really want it to be a love story, but a sort of funny love story. And it's not funny enough yet, is it? (*David goes to window, opens the curtains and looks out at Rodingham village.*)
DAVID. You know, darling, with this motorway and some hard work and a bit of luck, we Rodinghams might be here another five hundred years.
JULIE. (*Sits in desk chair.*) David! . . . The story.
DAVID. (*Turning from window.*) Hmmm? (*Going to Julie.*) What's the problem?
JULIE. It's not funny.
DAVID. (*Gaily.*) Well, make a list of all the crazy things that happened to *us* on the houseboat. Then twist them and exaggerate them. That's the way to get ideas! (*He spins her round in her chair so she faces the desk.*) You know I can just see you sitting here at your typewriter with the sun streaming in through this window—churning out *one successful story after another* . . . !

CURTAIN

AUDIO BRIDGE

(*Between Scenes 2 and 3 in Act II*)

Curtain falls on Scene 2.
Fade in sound of typewriter, hard at work. Phone starts ringing. Typewriter hesitates, then continues. Typewriter and phone ringing together for several seconds. Then typewriter stops. Pause. Julie answers phone.)

JULIE. Rodingham one two.
DAVID. (*Excited.*) Darling, I think we're in luck. Just heard that Longmeadow Farm is up for auction. It's only fifty acres, but it will start us off.
JULIE. When *is* the auction?
DAVID. In about three weeks, but . . .
JULIE. Then can't we talk about it later? I'm *so close* to getting this story right and the phone hasn't stopped all morning.
DAVID. Sorry, darling. But I'm just outside Tibbit's office and I'd

like him to bid for us. We may have to move fast. That news may
leak out any day.

JULIE. What news . . . ? (*Pause.*) Oh, you mean the motor . . . !

DAVID. Sssh—not on the phone, darling.

JULIE. (*Laughs.*) Oh, sorry! . . . All right, do whatever you
think best. But I *do* wish you could help me with this story tonight.
(*Sound starts to fade.*)

DAVID. I'll try but first things first. If I don't catch Tibbit now
I'll miss him altogether . . .

(Curtain rises on Scene 3)

ACT TWO

SCENE 3

TIME: *Several weeks later. Late afternoon.*

ALTERATIONS TO SET: *The dust sheets are gone. Also, the
pistols and their frames have been removed from the
study and this has left light silhouettes against the
darkened wallpaper which only emphasizes their absence.
On the study desk is Julie's typewriter. The library writing table is strewn with David's papers, including the list
of Julie's securities. This table has been turned at right
angles so that it faces R. On each side of it and facing
each other, are chairs C (L.) and B (R.).*

*Both rooms now have a tidier and more lived-in appear-
ance and there are flowers on the side table. Outside it
is a day of dark clouds and threatening rain, therefore
the landing lights and lamp on writing table are switched
on. Julie's small night case is in the hall.*

ON RISE: *David sits at writing table, hard at work. Then
he begins to search around in the table drawers (for the
red file).*

*Julie comes down the stairs. She is smartly dressed to go
to London, carries her purse, a raincoat and a copy of
the evening paper. Her anxiety and frustration have now
completely disappeared and she looks very attractive and*

50

*somewhat pleased with herself. She puts evening paper
on chair A and covers it with her purse and raincoat.*

DAVID. (*Looking up admiringly.*) Well, just look at her!

JULIE. (*Crossing to the desk.*) Thank you, darling! I do wish you
could come to London with me.

DAVID. Can't possibly. The auction is under way so I have to
stay by the phone. (*Searching through the desk again.*)

JULIE. What are you looking for?

DAVID. (*Still searching.*) That red file. I was just checking some
figures.

JULIE. Could it be in *my* room? (*She enters study.*)

DAVID. I always keep it in here. Don't you bother now. I'll find
it. (*As Julie goes to her desk, puts typewriter on floor and
straightens some papers amongst which is a typed manuscript.
They call across to each other, room to room.*)

JULIE. By the way, how did you like my *new* houseboat story?

DAVID. (*Hardly listening.*) Hmmm? Oh! Very good. (*As she
returns to study.*)

JULIE. (*In doorway.*) You never even read it!

DAVID. I most certainly did. (*She watches David as she stands
above writing table.*)

JULIE. The first two pages and then left it in the bathroom!

DAVID. (*Laughs.*) Sorry darling, but just as soon as we're in the
clear, I'll give you four hours every day. Meanwhile, we must get
some help. What was wrong with that couple you saw last week.

JULIE. (*Crossing R.*) She talked incessantly and he had a slipped
disk. And I can't listen to chatter and lift heavy things at the
same time, it makes me nervous. (*She is now standing above chair
A.*) By the way, have you seen the evening paper?

DAVID. (*He is busy at the desk and does not look up.*) Hasn't
arrived yet. You can buy one at the station.

JULIE. No, I've seen it. I just thought you might be interested.
(*But he still shows no interest.*) I think there was something about
your new motorway.

DAVID. (*Looking up sharply.*) Oh! Where did you put it?

JULIE. (*Vaguely.*) Hmm? Oh, I don't know. It's somewhere
about . . . (*She crosses to the library windows and looks out.*)
Is it going to rain? (*She suddenly notices something through the*

51

windows, off R. *Meanwhile David has left the table and is searching around for the evening paper. First he crosses to hall.*)
David? . . . Did you go into the other wing last night?
DAVID. Yes, I did, as it happens. Why?
JULIE. I thought I heard you. Why did you go there?
DAVID. (*As he crosses into study, glances around and then returns to writing table.*) I thought I saw a light in the guest room, but when I got there it was out. Must have been the moon on the window pane.
JULIE. There's a light there now. (*David leaves table, goes to Julie and looks through window.*)
DAVID. Are you sure you didn't switch it on?
JULIE. I haven't been up there for days.
DAVID. Well, don't miss your train. I'll have a look in a moment. (*They turn away from window.*)
JULIE. I get quite frightened when I'm alone here. You heard about Mrs. Clegg last summer? Two men walked in in broad daylight, tied her up and took both her . . . (*Phone rings.*)
DAVID. Off you go, darling. I'll phone you goodnight about ten. (*Into phone.*) Hello? . . . Oh, one moment, please. (*To Julie.*) It's for you. (*Julie takes phone. As David crosses to kitchen:*) Don't talk too long. I'm expecting a call from Mr. Tibbit. (*He exits into the kitchen. Julie talks quietly and excitedly with glances at kitchen door.*)
JULIE. Hello? . . . I have! And I'm on my way! . . . No, he has to stay here, so we'll meet as planned. You reserve a table. . . . No, Paul, I haven't told him. Let's see if he can find out for himself. That should teach him a lesson! I think the Rodinghams are inclined to take their women for granted! . . . Bye, my dear. (*She hangs up as David enters from kitchen carrying a tray with an electric coffee pot, cup and saucer. He takes these to the sideboard, and plugs in coffee pot. Meanwhile Julie crosses to chair A and picks up her things.*) I must fly. I'll take the Ford and leave it at the station. . . . (*She picks up her raincoat revealing the evening paper underneath.*) Oh! Here's your paper! (*David picks up paper, sits down and starts to look through it.*) Sure you don't want to come? . . . There's another train in an hour.
DAVID. Next week, darling. Have a good time. (*He kisses her.*)
JULIE. I will! (*She picks up her night case in hall and exits by front door.*)

DAVID. (*As an afterthought.*) Why not go to a theatre? (*Front door slams. Julie pauses on her way past window and peers in at David with a minx-like expression, as he turns the pages. Then she disappears* L. *The phone rings. David drops the paper on the floor, crosses and picks up the phone. Excitedly.*) Hullo. . . . Yes? (*Pause.*) Then you may have to go up to twelve thousand. . . . Good luck! (*During this phone conversation we see a shadow appear against the stairway wall as someone stands listening. David has his back to the stairway and doesn't notice. He hangs up the phone, leans over the table and makes a note on the· pad. A noise is heard upstairs. David looks up, startled and listens. Then he goes into study, opens second drawer and then bottom drawer of desk, takes out the silencer pistol and checks that it is loaded. While he is in study, footsteps are heard going down to the cellar. David tiptoes cautiously across library and creeps up the stairs, his pistol at the ready. A few seconds after David has disappeared at the top, the kitchen door slowly opens and Clive enters. He carries on a tray: a cold plate of chicken and salad, a wine glass, and three dusty bottles of burgundy, brandy and port. He strolls over to David's table and puts tray down. He turns and glances 'round at the stairway and we now see that the red file is in his left coat pocket. He takes it out and puts it back in the writing table drawer. Then he sits down to his meal, chair B. Just as he is pouring himself a little wine to taste, David bursts in from the kitchen. Seeing Clive, he immediately hides his pistol under his coat and stares at him, amazed and thoroughly embarrassed.*)

CLIVE. (*Half turning, very casually, hardly looking at David.*) Ah, David. (*Pause.*)

DAVID. How long have you been living with us?

CLIVE. (*Cheerfully.*) Flew in last night. (*As they talk, David picks up evening paper from floor and surreptitiously hides the pistol in the paper and puts it on chair* D D. R. NOTE: *During this scene Clive behaves in every way as though he was still master of Rodingham and, by every gesture, he just could not appear more at home.*)

DAVID. Where on earth have you been? You haven't written in months.

CLIVE. Yes, that was very remiss. However, I phoned Aunt Edie and she put me completely in the picture, as far as *your* activities are concerned. And, of course, I'm delighted! Don't misunderstand me, a most tragic business. Poor old Sturrock. But I do congratulate

53

you, David. As you know, this is what I've *always* wanted for you. (*As David crosses to the other side of his table and sits in chair C, facing Clive:*)

DAVID. Thank you, Clive. I'm afraid Julie's in London today, but we'd like you both to stay with us . . . for a bit.

CLIVE. Thank you, David. I'd like to.

DAVID. Your wife isn't with you?

CLIVE. (*As he eats and drinks.*) I'm afraid we are no longer together.

DAVID. I'm sorry.

CLIVE. Wasn't her fault, poor darling. I just should have taken those brothers into consideration.

DAVID. (*Amused.*) Oh, her brothers! Yes . . . she had six, if I remember?

CLIVE. Yes, there were six of them. And in six short words, they didn't like me—*at all.* Of course, they were violently prejudiced before I even arrived in Texas. They were all rooting for a childhood buddy of theirs called Elmer. Elmer was exactly like the brothers. In fact, I could never *quite* tell which were the brothers and which was Elmer. They would follow her around wherever we went, like Snow White and the Seven Dwarfs. Except they were all much bigger than me . . . and wore the most *enormous* hats! . . . Oh, I suppose I could have stayed and fought it out, but what a hope! Against six hostile brothers, a whole battery of family lawyers and eighty million dollars. And I was beginning to get a little short as it was.

DAVID. (*Horrified.*) Short? . . . Are you telling me that you have spent the entire proceeds from the sale of Rodingham? . . . In *one* year! (*Pause.*) Well? Go on—how much have you got left? (*Clive fishes deeply into his pocket as though feeling for small change. David gets the point immediately and rises.*) What on earth are you going to do now? (*As Clive talks on David goes to sideboard and pours himself coffee.*)

CLIVE. I must take pause. Find my bearings. Meanwhile—it's good to be home. (*Pause. David turns and glances ominously at Clive's back.*) Yes, there's a lot to be said for the gentler ways of living. And who knows? I might even take my seat in the House of Lords. Which reminds me, there's some talk of a new motorway . . . from London!

54

DAVID. (*Alarmed, turning from sideboard.*) Oh! Where did you hear that?

CLIVE. (*With a glance at the table drawer.*) Oh, I think I read it . . . somewhere. In a year or two I shall be able to drive up to Westminster in the morning, lunch in the Lords, debate . . . (*Yawns.*) and be back here in time for dinner. Life could be rather pleasant. (*David has now returned to* L. *of table with his coffee. Clive immediately takes the cup from David's hand.*) Oh, thank you, David . . . and I'll take a drop of brandy too, if you can find me a snifter . . . and I must tell old Liz I'm back. (*As Clive dials on phone, David takes brandy bottle to sideboard, finds a snifter, pours Clive's brandy and turns on lights [sideboard lamp and wall brackets].*)

DAVID. But they don't actually *pay* you anything in the Lords, do they?

CLIVE. Your point is well taken, David. That will be my little problem for a time. But I know you'll help me over the next stile —or two. (*Into phone.*) May I speak to Dr. Woolley, please . . . Yes it is! . . . Thank you, Nurse, it's good to be back! . . . Then would you ask her to phone me? . . . Yes, I'm at *home.* Goodbye, Nurse. (*Hangs up. David is on Clive's* R. *as he hands him brandy snifter and moves towards fireplace.*)

DAVID. Of course, we'll help you all we can, but I can't give you any money, Clive, I'm sorry.

CLIVE. (*With a laugh.*) Money? I don't think you quite understand me, I merely . . .

DAVID. Oh I understand you very well. And I want you to understand this. I myself have nothing. (*The phone rings. Clive picks it up quickly.*)

CLIVE. Well, hello, Liz! . . . Oh, I beg your pardon. For you, David.

DAVID. (*Crosses and takes phone.*) Hello. (*Pause. Clive moves below table and stands above chair* C, *glancing at papers on desk but also watching David with interest.*) Who are you up against? . . . When does it start? (*Quietly, turning away from Clive, who is watching him.*) Then go up to . . . Go as high as you need, but get it . . . And phone me. (*Hangs up. A pause.*)

CLIVE. You were saying . . . you have *nothing?*

DAVID. You see, this is Julie's house. And I don't want to seem academic, but these bottles which you just brought up from the cellar . . .

CLIVE. Are Julie's bottles as well. They are indeed. (*Laughs.*) Now you really don't mind my taking one bottle of port to Uncle Graham? I'm dining there tonight, you see. (*As he crosses slowly to chair A.*) But do tell me, David. If, as you say, this house and all these bottles and everything are all Julie's and in no way yours . . . how much *did* he leave her?

DAVID. I have no idea. (*Pause as Clive strolls thoughtfully to fire-place.*)

CLIVE. I suppose you could more or less work it out from a list of his securities.

DAVID. Yes, I suppose I could. (*Pause.*) But I haven't.

CLIVE. Oh then I think you *should.* (*Points at table.*) It's right there on your desk. I made it a shade under two hundred thousand pounds. Was that all? To hear him talk you'd have thought he had ten times as much. Poor old Sturrock. . . . You know, David . . . It's an odd sensation, standing here with everything just as it always was. I find it almost impossible to believe that it doesn't still belong to me.

DAVID. Well, I remember your being paid a substantial sum to realize that it doesn't!

CLIVE. Ah, but that was paid to me by Charles Sturrock. Money that he had well earned by virtue of the toil and sweat that he *personally* had excreted. But what did your Julie have to do with all that, hmm? No, I'm sorry, David, but this is still my home.

DAVID. I've always found your theories on the rights of property a little conflicting, Clive. But let me talk to Julie. Perhaps she'll see it your way.

CLIVE. Thank you, David. And now . . .

DAVID. But just suppose . . . that she says "No"? (*A long pause, then as Clive strolls slowly to the writing table and sits down in chair C.*)

CLIVE. Then I would have to come to my little brother, cap in hand, and ask for a job.

DAVID. I don't see how we could help you there. We've just en-gaged two gardeners and—you're not a particularly good cook, if I remember.

CLIVE. (*Slowly, leaning back in his chair.*) Then how about—Chairman and Managing Director of the Rodingham *Brothers*—

Estate—Development—Company—Limited? (*The phone rings.*) Let's see now, my turn, I think . . . (*Clive reaches for phone, but David snatches it up.*)

DAVID. (*Into phone.*) Yes? . . . Never mind about that. Did you get it? . . . Well done. See you tomorrow. (*Slams down phone and turns to Clive angrily.*) All right, where did you put it?

CLIVE. Where did I put what?

DAVID. I'm sorry you should find it necessary to pry into Julie's private files. . . .

CLIVE. I wasn't prying, David. I was actually looking for a copy of *Country Life*. Now, where would I have left it . . . ? (*He pretends to search for it.*)

DAVID. In your *room* perhaps?

CLIVE. No, no . . . of course, when *I* lived here I always kept important things in . . . (*Opens drawer and takes out file.*) Ah! . . . this it?

DAVID. (*Hesitates, then crosses to Clive.*) Just some old papers of Sturrock's. . . . We're still going through them. (*David reaches for red file but Clive withdraws it just out of his reach.*)

CLIVE. Oh, I see. Not planning to take over from where he left off by any chance?

DAVID. No, I'm *not!*

CLIVE. No, of course not. (*He opens file and turns pages.*) Then what are these scribbles in the margin . . . on almost every page? "Do this." "Check that." I see that against Sturrock's somewhat ominous note to "Buy Longmeadow Farm and *squeeze* out the Duke!"—you have pencilled in *today's* date! That is your writing, isn't it?

DAVID. This is really none of your business, but it's all perfectly legal.

CLIVE. Legal perhaps, but not exactly cricket, is it, old boy? At least, not the way we play it at Rodingham.

DAVID. All I'm trying to do is . . .

CLIVE. (*Laughs.*) Oh, it's quite clear what you're trying to do. You want to run a bulldozer over the village and turn their green pastures into a bloody suburb.

DAVID. That is not my intention at all. I want to stay here, preserve the manor and the village unspoiled. Keep a few hundred acres around us and build on the rest. With the income from that

I shall develop Rodingham until it can pay for itself. And that's all I want. I'm not out to make a killing and . . .

CLIVE. (*Interrupting.*) Thank you, David. You have just told me exactly what I wanted to know. But, of course, if I *do* come in with you, you'll have to do it *my* way.

DAVID. Your way!

CLIVE. Well, let's say, Sturrock's way. (*Holding up red file.*) This is the plan to make money. Why preserve the village? It's always been a dead loss. And what do you want to live *here* for? Make a marvelous clubhouse! I always said what this room needed was a long bar all the way from there to there.

DAVID. (*Angrily.*) You will have *nothing* to do with this!

CLIVE. Now David, we must learn to co-exist. After all, I am still Rodingham and titular head of this small community of simple country folk. Should I not warn them that there is a fox amongst the chickens? Why this very evening when Aunt Edie has left the table, I might have one too many glasses of—*Julie's* port and unfold to Uncle Graham this whole sordid scheme. (*David has moved to fireplace. He turns and faces Clive.*)

DAVID. (*Slowly.*) Clive, I'll give you ten thousand pounds . . . and you leave the country . . . for good.

CLIVE. You mean—like they did to Uncle Andrew? But where on earth would I go? And what would I do?

DAVID. Couldn't you *hawk* your title around the Bahamas or somewhere? I'm sure there must be other young girls with too much money, or even old ones!

CLIVE. Now you mustn't be cruel, David. Just because you've fallen on your feet—*for once.* Find myself a rich old girl, eh? (*Laughs.*) Incidentally, I meant to ask you . . . Julie and I . . . (*Pause.*) we *have* met . . . or haven't we?

DAVID. (*Puzzled.*) Of course you have. She was here that day you sold Rodingham.

CLIVE. (*As he sits on* D. *end of writing table.*) That's right. She was with *him*, wasn't she? Couldn't quite place her for the moment. Not as young as my late wife, if I remember . . . and perhaps not quite as striking a beauty . . . (*He picks up list of securities.*) But there are other advantages, aren't there? . . . All in her name, I see, and . . . Oh! . . . any brothers? (*Glances at David, who is standing very still.*) Mmmm! You're a lucky fellow, David. I sincerely hope that nothing will ever happen to make

58

her want to leave *you*. (*David has now reached his boiling point. The phone rings. Clive snatches it up.*)

CLIVE. Rodingham one two . . . Liz! My old sweetheart, how I've missed you . . . My marriage? . . . Not *particularly* successful . . . divorced . . . Yes. (*Laughs.*) Why not drop in here for a drink about seven and I'll tell you the whole sad story round by round. . . . (*As soon as Clive starts speaking, David picks up the pistol and newspaper and takes them into study. He goes to desk, drops newspaper into wastebasket and is about to put pistol into bottom drawer when Clive calls to him.*) Oh, but wait a minute! I was forgetting. This is *David's* house now, isn't it? (*Calling to David.*) David, do you think Julie would mind if Liz came for a drink tonight? . . . (*As David stands perfectly still, pistol in hand. A long pause.*) David!

DAVID. *Why not?*

CLIVE. (*Into phone, very cheerfully.*) Why not!—says David, beaming with hospitality! . . . Seven o'clock then? And over a glass of sherry we can decide exactly where I go from here. . . .

CURTAIN

ACT THREE

Scene 1

TIME: *The same evening.*

ALTERATIONS TO SET: *Both library and study are lit. Study curtains closed, library curtains open. Dark outside. Bang-contraption in position B-1 (out of sight). And the four pistols are now back on the wall in their frames. The battle axe is down and resting against the wall. The desk chair is under pistol frames. On the study floor, below the desk, lie two large shoes and, by them, a grocery bag. In library, David's table has been tidied (and red file removed).*

ON RISE: *The library window is open and David is by the sundial. He wears a pair of white cotton gloves. He is tense and working fast. He is scraping away a little cement at base of sundial into small tin with a cement trowel. Then he carefully tilts back sundial, shoves the trowel and cement tin into the hole underneath and lets sundial down again. He returns quickly to the library, closing window. As he goes to study, the phone begins to ring. He hesitates, then ignores it. He enters study, drops large shoes into grocery bag and takes it to desk. The phone stops ringing. A pile of Clive's mail, which includes one letter in a large envelope is on top of the desk. He takes a paper knife and quickly slits open three small letters and removes their contents (though he does not read them). Then he picks up the long envelope and is about to slit it open as well, then has an idea. Instead, he drops it into the grocery bag. There is the sound of a small car approaching and we see headlights against the library window. Sound of car door slamming, etc. David places the bag behind the study door.*

From the chest, he picks up the soda siphon, but after one squirt behind the chest he finds that it is empty. The phone starts ringing again. David takes siphon to sideboard. Then he answers the phone. As he crosses, he takes off the gloves.
David speaks politely, but impatiently.

DAVID. Hullo! . . . Oh yes, Nurse? . . . No, but I'm expecting her shortly . . . You're where? . . . The Yearsleys . . . What? . . . One three eight? (*He writes on phone pad, he glances around in time to see Dr. Woolley walk past the window.*) Yes, I'll tell her the moment she gets here. . . . Goodbye, Nurse. (*David hangs up. Front doorbell rings. Instead of answering door he goes quickly into study, drops gloves into grocery bag behind door, picks up the hammer and climbs onto the chair. After a few seconds, Dr. Woolley enters hall carrying her doctor's bag.*)

WOOLLEY. (*Calling.*) Clive! . . . David!

DAVID. (*Calling.*) In here, Liz. (*Woolley crosses to the study. David taps with hammer on the clip that holds the battle axe.*) Won't be a second. Do you mind handing me . . . (*Woolley puts her bag on desk and hands him the axe.*) Thank you. This nearly fell off the wall . . . Oops! (*As he lifts up axe, David deliberately knocks one of the pistol frames crooked. As David fixes axe on wall and straightens pistol frame.*) You didn't happen to notice anyone outside just now?

WOOLLEY. (*Missing the point completely.*) No, I didn't. Any phone calls?

DAVID. (*Hesitates, then vaguely as though not paying attention.*) Don't think so. That's better! (*As he climbs off chair and takes it to desk and offers Woolley a cigarette from the silver box:*) Clive should be back any minute. He's having tea with the Vicar. Cigarette? (*She picks one out, then drops it back again.*)

WOOLLEY. Thanks . . . Ugh! Filters! Julie home?

DAVID. No, she's in London searching for domestics. (*He lights cigarette from box.*)

WOOLLEY. Then while I have you alone, David, and at the risk of being told to mind my own damned business . . .

DAVID. Yes, Liz? (*David peers cautiously through study curtains.*)

WOOLLEY. Get out of this house! Young people should start from

61

scratch anyway. Can't put the clock back, can you? *Are you listening ?!*

DAVID. (*Quietly.*) Liz, switch the light off a moment—by the door.

WOOLLEY. What are you up to? (*She switches off light.*)

DAVID. Here, a second.

WOOLLEY. (*Goes and peeps through study curtains.*) What is it?

DAVID. By the box hedge, to the right. . . . It's a big man. Looks as if he's watching the house. I thought I saw someone out there just now. (*Looks toward the study door and sees Clive passing by the Library window. He carries bottle of brandy.*) Here's Clive anyway.

WOOLLEY. (*Turning from window.*) I can't even see the box hedge. Better phone the police, David. (*She enters library.*) I remember Rodingham when you didn't even have to lock your door. But crime pays these days. Poor old Mrs. Clegg! Locked her in the bathroom and took both her television sets. (*Clive enters from the hall. Meanwhile David takes a quick look around the study. He almost closes the study door. Then, very smoothly he takes the silencer-pistol from wall and drops it into the grocery bag. He starts to leave the room, then on a delayed reaction he goes back and collects Woolley's bag from the desk. He then enters the library closing the study door. He puts Woolley's bag on the floor by writing table. During above, Woolley greets Clive in library:*) Well, Clive! You don't look more than ten years older! (*Seeing the bottle of brandy he is carrying.*) Ah! Is this for me?

CLIVE. (*Wearily as he crosses to the sideboard.*) Yes, take it, please! (*Pours himself a large Scotch.*)

WOOLLEY. Very generous of you, Clive.

CLIVE. (*Bitterly.*) Don't thank me. Thank the Vicar. I was going to give it to him.

WOOLLEY. The devil you were! (*She sits chair A.*)

CLIVE. That man should have been a schoolmaster, not a clergyman. He had me standing in his study for over an hour. Like a small boy with my pants down. I've set an example to his entire parish. In the future, no marriage in Rodingham will last more than three months. (*He squirts soda at his glass, but as the siphon is empty, he holds it up to David.*) You're short on soda, David!

DAVID. Yes, I know! Glass of sherry, Liz?

WOOLLEY. Thank you. Well, come on, Clive. Now my interest

is strictly biological. Let's have it in a nut shell. *What* went wrong?
(*Clive crosses and sits in chair B, R. of writing table, and takes
a cigarette from his case. As they talk, he picks up a box of
matches from David's table but finds it is empty and tosses it
back. He then fishes in his own pockets, finds some cardboard
matches and lights his cigarette. David is pouring sherry and does
not see this.*)

CLIVE. Another time, Liz. I've discussed matrimony quite enough
for one day. I'll have to change in a minute. Dining with the
Duke. Any phone calls, David!

DAVID. (*Casually.*) No . . . but there was a large envelope for
you . . . from America.

CLIVE. Oh? . . . Where is it?

DAVID. (*Vaguely.*) Hmm? I put it with your others. (*Woolley
rises and crosses towards the study.*)

CLIVE. What others?

DAVID. They're—on the desk. (*Clive rises, moves L. of writing
table and searches for his letters.*) What do you want, Liz?

WOOLLEY. I think I left my bag in there.

DAVID. No, here it is. (*David picks up her bag from floor and
hands it to her. Then he guides her to chair B and hands her the
glass of sherry. She sits in chair B.*)

WOOLLEY. Oh thanks, David . . . Clive, did *you* notice anyone
outside just now? (*She puts her bag on table and starts digging in
it for a cigarette.*)

CLIVE. Notice who?

WOOLLEY. David thinks he saw a prowler.

CLIVE. (*With enthusiasm, crossing to hall.*) Then what are we
waiting for? It's three against one! Let's rout him out! David,
where do you keep those old pistols of father's?

DAVID. (*Hesitates.*) What pistols?

CLIVE. You know. The ones he used to hang on the wall in there.
(*A pause. Woolley takes a gulp of sherry.*)

WOOLLEY. They're still there.

CLIVE. Well come on then! (*Clive moves towards study but David
bars his way.*)

DAVID. Clive! . . . I wouldn't, if I were you.

CLIVE. Why not?

DAVID. Well—they aren't loaded for one thing and . . .

63

CLIVE. (*Pushing past David.*) What of it? We can still scare the hell out of him.

DAVID. Suppose he has a gun himself?

CLIVE. Don't be so windy. (*Opens study door.*)

WOOLLEY. (*Picking up phone.*) And don't you be childish, Clive! I don't mind if you two get knocked off. But I'm indispensable to this community. Let's see how long it takes our local constabulary to answer the call of duty. (*Dials "0."*)

DAVID. (*Looking on phone pad.*) Oh! Liz, I'm sorry, but there *was* a phone call for you.

WOOLLEY. When?

DAVID. Shortly before you arrived. Your nurse . . . she sounded in a bit of a flap. (*As they are speaking Clive has entered the Study, leaving the door open. David crosses to close curtains partway, watching Clive through the door. Clive glances at pistols, then turns and peeps through the study curtains. After peering out for a few moments he returns to the library. Meanwhile:*)

WOOLLEY. (*To David, annoyed.*) I asked you if there were any calls! (*Into phone.*) Doctor here! Hold on . . .

DAVID. The number's on the pad. The Yearsleys, I think.

WOOLLEY. Mrs. Yearsley! She's having a baby. If anything goes wrong with this I'll skin you alive. (*Into phone.*) Give me one three eight quickly . . . (*Seeing that Woolley is now occupied, David moves towards study, but Clive now re-enters Library and they almost bump into each other.*)

CLIVE. Can't see anyone. (*He resumes searching for his letters on David's table.*) You said my letters were on the desk? . . . David!

DAVID. (*Impatiently.*) No!—in there. (*Woolley has now found a cigarette and picks up box of matches from table, finding it empty she fishes for matches in her bag. Just as David enters study she asks him for a match.*)

WOOLLEY. (*Into phone.*) Hello, Tom. Doctor. Is Nurse there? . . . Got a match, David? (*Clive goes back into study, finds his letters on desk and starts to open them. David enters study and nearly closes the door. He picks up grocery bag [with his back turned to Clive], and when he turns to face him he is holding Clive's long envelope in his right hand. He then stands there with his back to door. Clive looks up from his mail.*) Well, Tom, I can't be everywhere at once . . . get Nurse to the phone. (*Continues searching for matches.*)

CLIVE. (*Sitting at the study desk.*) Did you open these?
DAVID. (*Quietly.*) Yes, I did. (*Holds out the long envelope.*) This is for you, as well.
CLIVE. *Why* did you open them?
DAVID. (*Coolly.*) You read my things. I read yours. (*Clive looks at David, first angrily and then suddenly laughs with amusement.*)
CLIVE. You know, David, I've always thought that I understood my little brother rather well. It now amuses me to discover that he is just beginning to understand *himself!*
DAVID. (*He is still holding out the long envelope invitingly.*) Well . . . it's never too late. (*Clive takes the envelope revealing the silencer-pistol which David is holding underneath it. Clive rises and backs to window. David fires and slams the door* [not very hard] *with his behind. Clive drops the letter and crumples up like a sack of potatoes. David catches him, spins him round and almost lays him on the floor. He then sets about to rig the Study so it appears to have been burgled. At the exact moment that David shoots Clive and slams the door, Woolley starts to speak on phone in library as follows:*)
WOOLLEY. All right, Nurse. Here I am. So what's the matter? (*Listens.*) One thing at a time, now. How's the mother, first of all? . . . Afibrinogenemia? . . . Yes or no? . . . No? . . . Then what are you fussing about? . . . What do you mean, it won't cry? Smack its bottom. . . . Well, smack it harder! We've been over this a hundred times. I know you. Don't just pat it, smack it! . . . Bring it over to the phone and smack it hard! (*Listens— pause.*) Well? Can you hear that?! . . . Now let me talk to the father. . . . (*Pause.*) Tom? (*Laughs.*) Well, how do you feel now? I don't know whether it's a boy or a girl, but I'll guarantee one thing—it's a baby! . . . No, she's fine. I'll be over in half an hour. Now give her a kiss, take a good shot of whiskey—and let me speak to Nurse again. (*Calling to study.*) Clive! Come in here . . . Clive! (*Action by David, in study, while Woolley is phoning as above. After shooting Clive and laying him down, David is so shocked by what he has done that he cannot remember what to do next. Then gradually he pulls himself together as he does the following:*
1. *He picks up grocery bag and drops in silencer-pistol.*
2. *He picks up long envelope, looks all over it for blood marks and then tosses it onto desk with other letters.*

65

3. *He takes bag to desk and drops in cigarette box.*
4. *He opens two desk drawers and scatters a few papers onto floor.*
5. *He takes bag to back wall and drops in the other three pistols.*
6. *He opens window wide, leaving curtains closed.*
7. *He hides bag outside window.*
8. *He hangs up bang-contraption [i.e., in sight of the audience as in diagram B-2] and then lights its cigarette. In lighting the cigarette David uses his own lighter from his pocket but in doing this he burns his fingers and drops his lighter onto the floor.*

Just as he starts to search for it Woolley calls from the Library: "Clive! Come in here . . . Clive!" This startles David and he decides to leave it there and goes quickly into library. While David is going through the above actions 1 to 8, he also mumbles to himself as though he was having a conversation with Clive, but what he says need hardly be heard and Woolley's dialogue on phone should be favored. This is what David says, while doing 1 to 8:)

DAVID. I posted a large batch of letters to your New York Bank about a week ago.

(CLIVE.) Anything important?

DAVID. I don't think so. Bills mostly. . . . And I paid a bill from your tailor's last Christmas.

(CLIVE.) Very good of you, old boy. How much?

DAVID. Over three hundred.

(CLIVE.) Remind me to give you that. . . . Don't forget now.

DAVID. No, I won't. (*As he returns to Library to join Woolley, he turns back and says to Clive, very casually.*) Come on, you can read those later. Liz has to go soon . . . hmm? . . . don't be so bloody rude. (*David closes door. Woolley hands the phone to David and says:*)

WOOLLEY. Here, listen to this, David. (*David listens to the phone.*) I spend half my life administering to all kinds of misery. This is what makes up for it! In all the world there's nothing more exciting than the outraged shouts of a newborn babe. Get Clive in here. (*Calling.*) Clive! (*David hands phone back to Woolley and crosses* D. R.)

DAVID. He's just opening his mail. He won't be a minute.

WOOLLEY. (*Into phone.*) All right, Nurse. I'll look in shortly. Everything under control now? (*She hangs up. She is still holding her cigarette.*)

DAVID. (*Absentmindedly.*) Let's see, we were just going to do something . . . now what was it? Oh yes, phone the police.

WOOLLEY. Yes, why don't you? (*As David goes to phone and dials 0 and waits.*) You know, I wanted Clive to hear that because that's exactly the noise he made. Every baby greets this world with his own signature tune. And they're as different as fingerprints. Now you were a cautious one, David. You weren't quite sure if you liked this world or not, but Clive gave a great shout of triumph! "Here I am, you lucky people!" (*As Woolley talks she wanders absentmindedly towards the study. David is still at the phone, waiting and does not notice this until she has almost reached the door. Then he stares after her in horror, too tongue-tied to speak. Then he slams the phone down almost knocking it over.*)

DAVID. (*Sharply.*) Where are you going?

WOOLLEY. (*Absentmindedly.*) Hmm? Where am I going? . . . Oh! (*Holds up cigarette.*) Get a match from Clive. (*Turns to door.*)

DAVID. I've got a lighter! Here. (*David feels in his pockets. Woolley wanders back a few paces towards him. Then David remembers that he dropped it in the other room. He looks around desperately, then sees box of matches on the table and snatches it up.*) Here you are!

WOOLLEY. No, that's empty. (*David opens box, Woolley turns and moves back towards study door and reaches for doorknob.*)

DAVID. It's all right. *Here's* my lighter! (*David pretends to find his lighter in his pocket. He masks it with his other hand as though to protect a weak flame and pretends to flick at it. Woolley moves slowly towards David.*)

WOOLLEY. (*Quietly.*) Have you got a chill, David? You're sweating a bit. (*Then impatiently, reaching for lighter.*) Oh come on! Give it to me. (*The bang-contraption goes off in the study and the pistol drops out of sight behind the chest. Woolley turns to study but does not move. David quickly moves between Woolley and the door.*)

DAVID. What the . . . ! (*Then quietly.*) Clive? . . . Are you all right? (*David turns door handle and pretends it is locked. Shouting violently.*) CLIVE! (*David rattles handle and throws his shoulder against door. Then he flings open library windows and curtains.*) Quickly, this way! (*Woolley follows David out onto* terrace. [*She must slam window shut as she exits.*] *A few moments later they enter at the study window, David first. David goes on his knees and turns Clive over.*)

WOOLLEY. (*Entering.*) Don't touch him! (*As Woolley goes down and examines Clive, David looks around and sees his lighter on the floor and quickly picks it up.*)

DAVID. (*Pointing at wall.*) The pistols! Someone's taken those pistols! (*But Woolley is only interested in Clive. David rushes to study door, rattles doorknob and then pretends to unlock it.*) .

WOOLLEY. David! He's gone. (*David stares at Woolley as if he doesn't believe her. Then he goes to wall, snatches down the battle axe, and runs to the window.*)

DAVID. (*Violently.*) Phone the police! Quickly! I'm going after him. (*Exits.*)

WOOLLEY. Don't be a fool! David! Come back! (*Woolley enters library and goes quickly to the phone and dials 0. As soon as Woolley picks up phone, David's hand appears through curtain in Study, unhooks bang-contraption and lifts it behind curtains. Shortly afterwards we see him appear by the sundial. He does the following in a very few seconds:*

WOOLLEY. (*On phone.*) This is Doctor. Give me the police station. . . . . Yes, quickly! (*Pause.*) Hello. Who is that? . . . Who? . . . This is Doctor Woolley. I'm at Rodingham Manor, Lord Rodingham has just been killed. . . . Someone broke into his study and shot him. . . . They took some firearms off the wall. . . . Just now. Not a minute ago. His brother and I were in the next room. . . . Mr. Rodingham thought he saw a man in the garden earlier this evening. He's gone after him. So you better hurry. . . . How soon can you . . .

1. *He lays grocery bag on ground by sundial.*

2. *He tips sundial over onto one edge.*

3. *He shoves the bag into hole underneath.*

4. *He lowers sundial back into position and leans on it heavily.*

As he does all this he keeps peeping through the window at Woolley as she phones. Then David rushes into library, heavily out of breath and snatches the phone from Woolley.)

DAVID. (*Panting hard and very fast.*) Hello! Police? This is

68

David Rodingham. . . . I think he got away in a car. I saw one drive out of our lane and go towards the London Road. . . . That's right. . . . No, no, no! The *other* way, the *other* way . . . !

CURTAIN

ACT THREE

SCENE 2

TIME: *Early the following morning.*

ON RISE: *The library and study curtains are open. The lights in both rooms are out. Heavy rain has been falling outside, and at the moment it is just beginning to get light. In the study, Clive's body has been removed but on the carpet is a patch of blood. Otherwise, the police have left the room exactly as it was at the time of the murder, i.e., the drawers of desk are still pulled out, papers still scattered on floor etc.*

A uniformed Police Constable is on guard outside and walks a slow beat from the library window to the study window and back. He wears a rain cape.

David enters from kitchen. He carries a tray on which is a coffee cup and an electric coffee pot, which he plugs in by sideboard. Then he picks up the phone and dials 0. (He does not yet notice the Police Constable outside.)

DAVID. (*Anxiously.*) Will you try Hyde Park 8282 again, please? (*He hangs up and crosses to study. He opens door, peers inside. He looks around the room thoughtfully and is about to leave when he notices again the patch of blood. He takes the evening paper, which is still in wastebasket, by desk, opens it up and spreads it over the carpet to hide the bloodstain. At this moment the Police Constable appears outside Library window from R. and for a moment peers at David curiously [i.e. through library window and study door]. The phone rings in library. David returns to Library, closes door and answers phone. During phone call the Police Constable only glances in casually as he continues his beat.*)

DAVID. Hello . . . Berkeley Hotel? Mrs. David Rodingham, please. (*Pause.*) I can't believe she hasn't been in all night! Are

69

you sure? . . . Hasn't she phoned? . . . Well, if she does . . . (*He now notices the Police Constable crossing on the terrace and lowers his voice.*) If she does, please ask her to call her husband . . . at home. It's quite urgent. Thank you. (*David hangs up and opens library window and calls:*) Officer! (*The Police Constable appears from the* L.)

POLICE CONSTABLE. Yes, me Lord!

DAVID. I had no idea you were still out there. Do come in.

POLICE CONSTABLE. (*Entering.*) Very kind of yer, me Lord. (*The Police Constable is a faithful "old sweat," kindly, unambitious and deferential.*)

DAVID. Take your cape off.

POLICE CONSTABLE. Beggin' yer pardon, me Lord, but best not to touch nothin' in there. I was meant to tell yer.

DAVID. No, of course. There was some blood on the carpet so I just spread some paper over it. I didn't want my wife to see it.

POLICE CONSTABLE. (*Taking off his cape.*) That's right, you wouldn't want that.

DAVID. By the way, when my wife gets home—would you please *not* mention anything about—last night. Not until I've spoken to her. It will be rather a shock.

POLICE CONSTABLE. It will be, I'm sure. 'Corse she may 'ave 'eard it on the radio. I didn't 'ear the seven o'clock news meself.

DAVID. I did. It wasn't mentioned.

POLICE CONSTABLE. And then it'll be in the mornin' papers . . .

DAVID. I think if she *had* heard anything she'd have phoned me by now. Do sit down. (*The Police Constable perches on chair B. David crosses to the sideboard.*) I'm just making some coffee. I expect you could do with some, too.

POLICE CONSTABLE. Thank you kindly, me Lord, but—er—not just now. Some of the ladies from the village set up a tea wagon at one of the road blocks last night. I took on so much I was just about floatin'.

DAVID. (*Pouring his coffee.*) Oh . . . if you want to go anywhere, it's the third door on the left.

POLICE CONSTABLE. I'm—'er—all right now, me Lord. Took the liberty while I was out there, beggin' your pardon . . . (*David sits in chair A. Has coffee cup with him.*) Gaw! Last night wasn't 'alf a shambles! The 'ole village was millin' around. Women and children as well. And then the old Duke turns up with 'is gun and 'is dogs an' starts to reorganize things. And then . . . (*Laughs.*) . . . then they brings the blood'ounds over from Wopping Dean in a milk van! (*Pause. This is one thing David never thought of.*)

DAVID. Bloodhounds?

POLICE CONSTABLE. That's right, me Lord. We found some large footprints in the garden. So someone suggests they bring the blood'ounds over 'ere and let 'em take a niff around and see where it lead 'em. (*Pause.*)

DAVID. Any . . . luck?

POLICE CONSTABLE. Well, yer see, blood'ounds is very sensitive animals. And no sooner was they out of the van and signed for, than the Duke's dogs was at 'em and they was chasing each other around in the dark till two in the morning!

DAVID. They'll try the bloodhounds again today, I expect.

POLICE CONSTABLE. Too late now. The rain will 'ave killed any scent there was.

DAVID. (*Leans back in his chair, much relieved.*) What beats me is how anyone can do a thing like this and get away with it. And so easily.

POLICE CONSTABLE. Don't you worry, me Lord. We'll get 'im all right.

DAVID. That's all very well—but will you? (*The phone rings. David rises, crosses to phone.*) Hello? (*Pause.*) Yes he is. (*To the Police Constable.*) It's for you.

POLICE CONSTABLE. (*Taking the phone.*) Constable Hackett. (*Suddenly springs to attention.*) Sir!! (*He stands at ease as if he had been ordered to do so.*) Sorry, sir. (*He puts one hand over ear as if straining to hear what's being said.*) A little louder, sir. (*Slight pause as the caller speaks again.*) Yes sir. (*Long pause. David extremely tense.*) No questions, sir. (*He hangs up. Long pause during which Police Constable goes and puts on cape, then finally David asks, as casually as possible:*)

DAVID. Any . . . news?

POLICE CONSTABLE. That was jus' the police station, givin' me the tip-off. There's a Detective Inspector and a Sergeant coming down from Scotland Yard on the first train.

DAVID. I see. (*Pause.*) But . . . why Scotland Yard? (*Sound of car coming up the drive. Car door slams.*)

POLICE CONSTABLE. 'ere they are now! (*Peering through window.*) No, it ain't. It's Lady Rodingham!

DAVID. *Who?!* (*A moment later Julie runs past the window. She carries her night case and a small parcel. David opens window and tries to hustle the Constable out.*)

POLICE CONSTABLE. An' best not to touch nothin' in there, me Lord. Not till they get 'ere.

DAVID. No, no. I won't go in there at all, and thank you. (*Constable exits by library window and disappears* L. *David closes the window. Julie enters from hall, surprised and delighted to see David and throws her arms around his neck and kisses him. David, however, is very grave.* NOTE: *In this last scene, Julie is bright and very happy for she believes she has done something which will please David very much.*)

JULIE. Darling! Up so early! (*Laughs. Brushes him off.*) Oh, sorry! Now I've made you all wet! (*David moves to hall, speaking quietly and calmly.*)

DAVID. Come upstairs, darling. I've got to tell you something. (*But Julie does not sense the situation and takes off her raincoat.*)

JULIE. Is that coffee hot? I had to miss breakfast. (*As she crosses to pour coffee she glances briefly at David.*) Now don't be angry, darling. I know I should have phoned you last night, but things were happening *so fast!*

DAVID. (*From portal on stairs.*) But where were you?

JULIE. With Paul and Margot Weiner. I took them out to dinner. Then we sat up till about three talking about it, so they finally made me stay the night.

DAVID. (*Coming down the stairs and into the room.*) But . . . how did they know about this?

JULIE. They read it, of course. Absolutely everybody's reading it. And talking about it too. (*As she crosses to* R. *of writing table and tries to open package containing material samples.*) And on the train this morning, there were two men discussing it practically the whole way from London. Of course, I was just dying to tell them who I was. . . .

DAVID. (D. R.) Julie, I don't know what you're talking about!

JULIE. (*Turning to him.*) And I don't understand you. Not at all! . . . (*Suddenly realizing.*) Don't tell me you didn't . . . ! *You haven't even read it!* Oh, darling! And I wanted you to find it yourself! (*Looking around for the newspaper.*) Now I bet you've thrown it away. Oh, well! (*Turning to David.*) I won that competition, that's all. First prize!

DAVID. What competition?

JULIE. In the Evening News. The same one as last year. (*Turning to package on table, her back to David.*) You see I thought if I could try for it again with a completely *new* story it might help to—close the door. But then I . . .

DAVID. (*Interrupting.*) Julie! . . . (*Gently.*) This was your . . . houseboat story?

JULIE. (*Turning to David.*) No. You see . . . well, it just wasn't funny! And I didn't have time to get it right— (*Crossing to other side of table, opening drawer, taking out scissors and opening package.*) so I put in our old one. And you know that worked even better! I seemed to write the whole thing completely out of my system and when you read it I think you'll feel the same way. (*As she continues talking, David leaves her and enters the study. He goes down on his knees and turns the pages of the evening paper which is spread on the floor. Sound of car coming up drive, halting, two car doors slamming. As Julie continues speaking, she takes out sample materials and lays them over the chairs.*) I know I'll be all right now. And I'm sure I can be happy here after all! It's not exactly my idea of home—but when we've knocked out that wall and redecorated this room completely—and thrown out that arsenal and all these stuffed animals and . . . (*As she takes some fabric to the window she notices two men appear on the terrace from the L. She watches them for a moment then calls through the study door.*) David! . . . It's the two men on the train! (*She goes into the study. David is still reading her story on the floor. She glances at the open drawers in desk, and the empty pistol frames, then stares blankly at David and as he slowly rises to his feet, still holding the newspaper with both hands, we see a large smear of blood on the bottom sheet, and as he turns to face Julie, she sees it as well. Meanwhile, the two men from Scotland Yard are inspecting the sundial. The Senior Officer keeps referring to a damp copy of an evening paper which he also holds with both hands. The Younger Officer tries to move the sundial but it is stuck fast. The Constable appears carrying a hammer and chisel. He strikes at the cement at the base of the sundial with a mighty "Clang!" And then another . . . and then another . . . Julie turns around sharply at the first "Clang" . . . then slowly back to David. They stand quite still and stare at each other.*)

SLOW CURTAIN
73

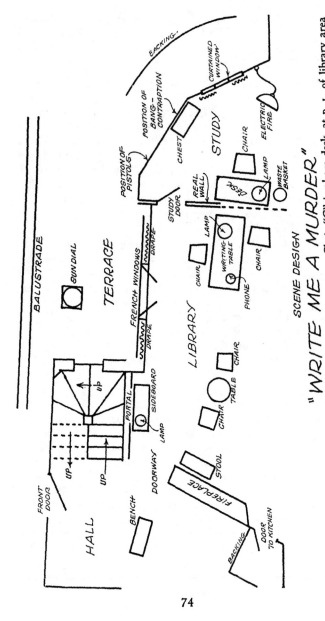

"WRITE ME A MURDER"

SCENE DESIGN

Chair "A" is one at R. of round side table at D. R.   Chair "C" is above desk, at D. L. of library area
Chair "B" is on opposite side (L.) of round side table at D. R.   Chair "D" is below desk, at D. L. of library area

DESCRIPTION OF THE SET
(see also diagram of the scene design)

(Left and right means the actor's left and right)

THE LIBRARY AND STUDY OF RODINGHAM MANOR

The manor has been the country seat of the Rodinghams for five hundred years and is now in a most dilapidated condition.

These two rooms are the den of an English country squire. The library is the much larger room on the right. The study is a very small room on the left. They are separated by an imaginary wall which is represented by a real door at the back and a few feet of wall to represent the rest.

The Library

In the back wall are large French windows. Through these we can see a narrow terrace on which there is a sundial. Above the sundial is a balustrade and beyond that a drop showing the distant country side (winter). Up right is the open *hall doorway* leading to the hall and the front door. A stairway leads upstairs from the hall and part of this can be seen through a large opening in the back wall (this opening is referred to as "the portal"). In the right wall is an open fireplace. Down right is a door leading to the kitchen and the servants' quarters. Against the back wall and underneath the portal is a sideboard on which there is a table lamp. Down centre is a writing table on which there is a table lamp and a telephone. There are four chairs in the Library; chairs A, B, C and D—(for their positions see the scene design). Only chair A has arms, and it is nearest to the fireplace and is the most important in appearance. Between chairs A and B is a round side-table on which there is an ashtray. There may also be a low footstool close to chair A. In the hall, opposite the front door and out of sight, is a bench on which coats can be tossed. Above the fireplace hangs a portrait of the first Baron Rodingham. Also on the walls and around the room may be several heads of big game and other trophies. The bracket lights over the fireplace and the lamp on the sideboard can be controlled from a switch by the hall doorway. The hall and stairway are separately lit.

The Study

In the left wall is a single French window. Above this window and against the left wall is a small narrow chest of drawers. (The "bang-contraption" will be hung over this chest and will fall behind it—see separate notes in back). An electric heating stove is plugged into a socket in the wall in the corner down left. Down right is a desk and a chair (study chair). On the desk is a table lamp, silver cigarette box, etc. Hanging on the wall, up left, is a collection of four modern pistols of various types. The one that is lowest and nearest to the door is fitted with a long silencer. Each pistol is mounted, with clips, into a wooden frame. Above the pistols and also on the back wall hang various relics of the past such as: an ancient battle axe, swords, a tattered battle flag, etc. The study bracket light and the desk lamp are both controlled from a switch below the door.

In both rooms the darkened wall paper is peeling off in places and the ceiling (if any) is cracked. Heavy full length curtains can be drawn over the windows in both rooms.

Note 1. For the simplification of stage directions, the *French* windows in both rooms are referred to, throughout the play, as "the Library (or Study) windows."

Note 2. As there is little room for bookshelves on the walls of the larger room (i.e. the Library)—it must be assumed that the books are in the "fourth wall." This will not confuse the audience as this room is only referred to as "the Library" in stage directions but never in the dialogue.

Note 3. Re the *fire.* In the Broadway production it was possible to use a device with real flames in which the copies of the story were actually burned. In London this was not allowed and so the most realistic effect was produced by using an iron stove set inside the open fireplace and a lighting device inside the stove. A possible alternative to these arrangements would be to angle the right wall so that no part of the audience could see into the fireplace and to use a lighting device to indicate the burning of paper.

Note 4. Re the *sundial.* At least part of it must be seen by everybody in the audience. To facilitate this it may be necessary:
a. for some furniture in the Library, i.e. the writing table and most of the chairs—to be not too solid, i.e. so that the position of the sundial can be seen *through* or under the furniture.
b. for the outside terrace and the base of the Library windows to be raised two or three steps.
The sundial can be any shape but it must have a square base—so that it can be tipped on its edge without losing its alignment.

Note 5. In order that the entire audience may see the "bang-contraption" it may be necessary, in some theatres, to modify the set design by building the left and back walls of the Study at more of an angle, so that the position of the bang-contraption may be brought further to stage right—even at the cost of making the Library slightly **smaller.**

DESCRIPTION OF THE "BANG-CONTRAPTION"
(See diagrams)

Only three people need understand the bang-contraption: David, the Director and the member of the stage management who works it off stage (S.M.) (The audience will have only a vague idea of how it works and that will be quite sufficient.)

First you must understand:

A. How it is *supposed* to work—theoretically.

and then

B. How it is *cheated* in the play.

A. *This is what is supposed to happen.*

(See diagrams A-1, A-2 and A-3)

A revolver is loaded with a blank cartridge. Attached to the gun are two pieces of string (S and L). The Shorter string is tied in a slip knot around the butt. The Longer string is tied, in a noose, around the trigger and the trigger guard. Both strings have loops (S and L) at their other ends and these both hang from a small nail in the wall (see diagram A-1). Also tied into the Shorter string is an ordinary cigarette. When this is lit it burns like a fuse until it reaches and burns through the Shorter string. The revolver is then supported only by the Longer string and drops down and out of sight behind the chest. The noose tightens around the trigger and the gun is fired. (See diagram A-3.)

There is one other position (see diagram A-2). This is used when David lights the bang-contraption. In order to do this he must raise it up from behind the chest. He does this by hanging the revolver from another loop (X) which is tied in the Shorter string between the cigarette and the loop S. It will be seen from the diagrams A-1 and A-3, that when the revolver is hanging from either loops S or L—the revolver is out of sight behind the chest but that when it is hanging from loop X the revolver is raised into the third position for lighting, i.e. against the wall above the chest (see diagram A-2).

(See "B" for how it is done in the play.)

77

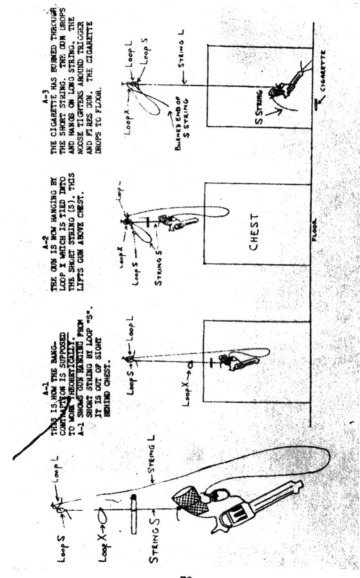

A-1

THIS IS HOW THE BANG-CONTRAPTION IS SUPPOSED TO WORK THEORETICALLY. A-1 SHOWS GUN HANGING FROM SHORT STRING BY LOOP "S". IT IS OUT OF SIGHT BEHIND CHEST.

Loop S

Loop L → Loop L

Loop X → O

A-2

THE GUN IS NOW HANGING BY LOOP X WHICH IS TIED INTO THE SHORT STRING (S). THIS LIFTS GUN ABOVE CHEST.

Loop L

Loop X

Loop S

String S

CHEST

A-3

THE CIGARETTE HAS BURNED THROUGH THE SHORT STRING. THE GUN DROPS AND HANGS ON LONG STRING. THE NOOSE TIGHTENS AROUND TRIGGER AND FIRES GUN. THE CIGARETTE DROPS TO FLOOR.

Loop L

Loop S

Loop X

Burned End of S String

S String

String L

Loop S

Loop L

Loop X → O

String L

String S

CIGARETTE

FLOOR

78

B. *This is how it is cheated in the play.*

(See diagrams B-1, B-2 and B-3)

Both strings are made of black nylon fish line which is thin, strong and practically invisible against the dark study wall.

The lower end of the Longer string is tied *permanently* to the trigger guard *only* (it will appear to be noosed around the trigger as well). At its other end loop L is hooked over the nail in the wall.

One end of the "Shorter" string (string S) is tied around the butt of the pistol with a slip knot—but there is no loop S at the other end because this "Shorter" string is not hooked over the nail at all but passes through a small hole in the wall about two inches left (upstage) of the wall nail. This S string is manipulated by the S.M. from the other side of the wall. He must be able to control the revolver on the other side in three positions:

B-1—when the revolver is hanging out of sight behind the chest and *before* the cigarette is lit.

B-2—when it is raised above the chest for lighting the cigarette.

B-3—when the cigarette is supposed to have burned through the S string.

In the latter case—when the S.M. receives the cue he simply lets the S string fall through the hole as far as it will go. The revolver will then drop until it is hanging behind the chest from loop L (see diagram B-3). At the same time (or to be exact—one second later) the S.M. fires a second revolver off stage.

David and the S.M. must practice together so as to be able to change smoothly from positions B-1 to B-2 and/or back again, i.e. when David raises the revolver from B-1 so as to light the cigarette—the S.M. will feel the string go loose and must take in the slack until it hangs in position B-2. Alternatively when David pulls downwards the S.M. must let out the string until it is in position B-1.

After the Bang the S.M. opens the trap door behind the chest and does the following:

1. With a pair of scissors he cuts the string S just above and below the cigarette and removes the cigarette.

2. He drops another (wet) cigarette on the floor.

3. He closes the trap door.

In order to control the string on the off stage side—the S.M. should wind it under a nail several inches underneath the hole in the wall and then secure it around a second nail several inches to the right. He should also mark, with white crayon on the black string, the various positions B-1, B-2, etc., as a guide.

THIS IS HOW IT IS CREATED IN THE PLAY

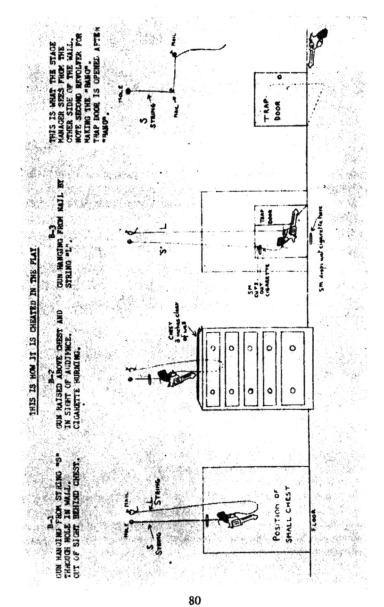

B-1
GUN HANGING FROM STRING "S" THROUGH HOLE IN WALL. OUT OF SIGHT BEHIND CHEST.

B-2
GUN RAISED ABOVE CHEST AND IN SIGHT OF AUDIENCE. CIGARETTE BURNING.

B-3
GUN HANGING FROM NAIL BY STRING "L".

THIS IS WHAT THE STAGE MANAGER SEES FROM THE OTHER SIDE OF THE WALL. NOTE SECOND REVOLVER FOR MAKING THE "BANG". TRAP DOOR IS OPENED AFTER "BANG".

POSITION OF SMALL CHEST

FLOOR

TRAP DOOR

TRAP DOOR

SM drops real cigarette here

SM cuts no. 2 out cigarette here

CHEST 3 inches clear of wall

HOLE

NAIL

S STRING

L STRING

S STRING

NAIL

NAIL

NOTES ON THE SILENCER-PISTOL

It will be obvious that, for the purposes of this play, the noise from the silencer-pistol must not exceed the sound of a slamming door. This point is mentioned because a real blank fired with a real silencer (and particularly in a theatre) is liable to give a surprisingly loud report.

If a real silencer is used it should be packed with steel gauze. A very small amount of Fuller's earth in the end of the gauze will produce a "smoking" effect when the pistol is fired. Only a pistol can be used with a real silencer. A revolver will not work as the sound will escape through the revolving mechanism.

An air-pistol will produce about the correct amount of noise and a little Fuller's earth in the barrel will provide the "smoking."

It will be noted that the silencer-pistol is, in fact, only fired twice in the play. Firstly when David is demonstrating it to Julie in I-2 and secondly when he kills Clive in III-1 and *on both occasions the door is slammed at the same time.* Therefore the simplest method of all would be for David merely to pretend to fire the pistol as he slams the door. If this latter method (or an air pistol) is used—a dummy silencer will be quite sufficient. This can easily be made of painted (grey-black) metal or even wood. It should be 4 or 5 inches long and securely attached to the barrel of the pistol.

PROPS

ON STAGE: LIBRARY

Swords and shield—on wall—above D.R. kitchen door.

Oil portrait in gold frame—on wall—between swords and door frame.

Hand bellows—D. end of fireplace.

Rack with Long Handle Fireplace Shovel—D. end of fireplace.

Fireplace
　Andirons
　Poker
　Concrete logs
　Sterno

Fireplace mantle
　Small wooden box with gold decor—D.
　Large wooden box—C.
　Small wooden box with gold decor—U.

Oil portrait of the First Baron Rodingham in gold frame—on wall—above mantle.

Footstool—U. end of fireplace.

Tiger head—on wall—above entrance to the hall—U.R.

Trophy cup—(tarnished)—on ledge or door frame—entrance to the hall U.R.

Bench—in hall with bang contraption—black string attached to trigger—loop on other end.

Highback chair—in hall—R. of door.

Oil portrait in gold frame—in hall—on wall—R. of door.

Shield with crossed swords—in hall—on wall—R. of door.

Sideboard—U.R.
　On top:
　　Picture—L.—leaning against wall
　　Table lamp—R.
　　Ash tray with water—L.
　　Matches—L.
　　Sherry bottle—L.C.
　　Tea box with teaspoon
　Inside:
　Top shelf:

Port glasses—L.
Sherry glasses—next
Brandy snifters—next
Highball glasses—R.
Bottom shelf:
Brandy bottle—L.
Siphon bottle—next
Vermouth bottle—next
2 Scotch bottles—R.
Many liquor bottles—back of bottom shelf (for dressing)
Big throne chair—with arms—L. of fireplace—on black marks.
Round table—left of big throne chair
Matches
Ash tray
Small ornament
2 books
Small throne chair—on black marks—R. of C.
Red cushion (no arms)
Library desk—C.
On top:
Cigarette box with cigarettes
Matches
2 ash trays with water
Lamp—U.L. end
Telephone—U.—R. of lamp
Pad of paper
Pencil
Ink well
Pens
Roll blotter
Empty sherry glass—U.
In D.R. drawer:
Scissors
Papers
Gray envelope
In D.L. drawer:
Papers
Wastebasket—under L. end of desk.
Desk chair—above desk—pushed under R. end of desk.
Small upholstered chair—with arms—below desk—set at an angle.
Bear's head—on wall—over door leading to study.
Faded red velvet drapes and valance—U.C.
Library drapes—(open)

Two oil paintings in gold frames—above door leading to library.
Key—in door between study and library.
Shelf with books—u. well—l. of door.
Two framed photographs—on wall—below shelf.
Study desk—l.c.
  On top:
    Desk blotter
    Desk lamp—u.r. end
    Silver cigarette box with filters
    Commando-knife letter opener
    Silver vase with pencils
    Ash tray
    Matches
  In drawers:
    Papers, letters, newspaper clippings, files, index cards, used envelopes, etc.
Wastebasket—d. of study desk.
Swivel desk chair—l. of study desk.
Stove—u.l.—with stove pipe going to ceiling.
Boar's head—on wall—above and to the r. of stove—or above light bracket.
Small coal shovel—on wall—l. of stove.
Small coal poker—on wall—l. of stove.
4 pistols in frames—on wall—including silencer with primers, Fuller's earth (bottom frame)
Small chest—u. of garden door (or French window)
Small framed photograph—on wall—above small chest.
Battle axe—on wall—above chest.
Crossed spears and swords—on wall—u. of chest.
Rigging for bang contraption set with cigarette noose—hanging behind chest.
Dead cigarette—on floor—under chest.
Tattered battle flag—on wall—above d.l. garden door.
Small table—d.l. below garden door—with empty brass urn.
Small rug—d.—without blood.
Faded red velvet drapes—garden door d.l. (or French window)
Study drapes—(Open)
Study door—(Open)

TERRACE

Sun dial—c.—hinged on r. side.
Shutters—tied back—l. of l. window
  Hinged onto l. window—4 hinged sections.

Actors pick up the following props:

Candelabra with one candle lit—David—Act 2—Scene 2
Tray—David—Act 2—Scene 3
  Coffee cup, saucer, teaspoon
  Coffee pot
    Electric cord—attached
    Hot coffee
  Sugar bowl with sugar
  Cream pitcher with milk.
Actors pick up the following props:

Tray (Clive) Act 2—Scene 3
  Plate of cold chicken, lettuce, tomato.
  Port glass
  Dusty burgundy bottle—cork almost out
  Dusty brandy bottle—cork almost out
  Dusty port bottle—cork in
  Knife and fork
  Napkin
Red file (Clive) Act 2—Scene 3
  Map
  Upstairs:
Canvas stool

LONDON EVENING NEWS (Julie) Act 2—Scene 3.

Crew sets the following props from the right:

Tray (to sideboard) Act 1—Scene 2
  Tea pot—R.; spout U. 2 cups and saucers
  Sugar bowl with sugar; cream pitcher with milk
  2 teaspoons
Electric kettle with boiling water (to sideboard) Act 1—Scene 2
Bullet (to library desk) Act 1—Scene 2
Story (to library desk) Act 1—Scene 3
Brass bowl of flowers (to round library table) Act 2—Scene 2
Pile of mail with list of securities in long heavy manila envelope on top
  (to D. or U.R. door in hall) Act 2—Scene 2
2 dust sheets
  (one over R. throne chair and round table) Act 2—Scene 2
  (one over chair D.R.) Act 2—Scene 2
David's 2 books, list of securities, papers with figures (to library desk)
  Act 2—Scene 3
Empty match box (to library desk) Act 3—Scene 1
Cement trowel (to sundial) Act 3—Scene 1

Cement tin with cement (to sundial) Act 3—Scene 1
White gloves (to sundial) Act 3—Scene 1

OFF LEFT

Actor pick up the following props:

Bicycle—(David) Act 1—Scene 1
Knapsack (David) Act 1—Scene 1
Typewritten letter and carbon copy (Charles) Act 1—Scene 1
Large suitcase (Charles) Act 1—Scene 4
Small suitcase (Julie) Act 1—Scene 4, Act 3—Scene 2
Typewriter case (Julie) Act 1—Scene 4
   Typewriter
   Manila envelope with story (envelope unsealed, addressed and
     stamped)

Actors pick up the following props:

Attache case (Charles) Act 1—Scene 4
   4 books
   Pint whiskey bottle
Thin leather briefcase (Charles) Act 1—Scene 4
   Red file with map, papers (together)
   Check book—in a side compartment of case.
Small wrapped parcel (Julie) Act 3—Scene 3
   2 samples of fabric. (Parcel tied with heavy cord)
London Evening News (Scotland Yard Man) Act 3—Scene 2
Flashlight (Scotland Yard Man) Act 3—Scene 2
Coal hammer and chisel (Police Constable) Act 3—Scene 2

Crew sets the following props from the left:

Off stage gun with blanks for bang-contraption sound Act 1—Scene 2,
   Act 3—Scene 1
Grocery (paper) bag with Wollock's Groceries, Ltd., Rodingham—
   printed on one side of bag. (to floor below desk) Act 1—Scene 2
   Large man's shoes—inside bag.
Hammer (to chest) Act 1—Scene 2, Act 2—Scene 1, Act 3—Scene 1.
2 dust sheets
   (one to cover library desk and u. desk chair) Act 2—Scene 2
   (one to cover chair R. of library desk) Act 2—Scene 2
Julie's glasses (to study desk) Act 2—Scene 3
Typewritten pages (to study desk) Act 2—Scene 3
Fern (to brass urn on small round study table) Act 2—Scene 3
Clive's 3 letters and large gray U.S. envelope (to study desk) Act 3—
   Scene 1
Cloth shopping bag (to below desk) Act 3—Scene 1
Rug with blood (to floor—D.L.) Act 3—Scene 2

Water sprayer (to wet down actors off L.) Act 3—Scene 2
Red Cado ink—for blood Act 3—Scene 2

PERSONAL

CLIVE:
Gold cigarette case with cigarettes.
Gold lighter
Matches

DAVID:
Zippo lighter
Cigarettes
Cigarette lighter
Matches
Wrist watch

DR. WOOLLEY:
Doctor's bag with:
    Glass needles
    Plastic capsules
    Cotton
    Bottle of alcohol
    Cigarettes
Wrapped in
white
flannel

JULIE:
Purse with note
Purse with pad, pencil
Umbrella

CHARLES:
Checkbook
Fountain pen
Newspaper clipping
Fountain pen in smoking jacket.

MR. TIBBIT:
Notebook
Pencil.

END OF ACT 1—SCENE 1

Strike:
Typewritten letters (from library desk) to off; used sherry glass (from library desk) to off

Set for Act 1—Scene 2:
Move big throne chair to red marks.

Move footstool to red marks.
Electric kettle to sideboard—plugged into outlet
Tray with tea pot, sugar bowl, spoons
On sideboard 2 cups and saucers, milk pitcher
Small throne chair to red marks.
Bullet on R. end of library desk.
Soda siphon—from sideboard to U.C. of library desk.
Small chair below desk—set so it faces R.
Put sherry bottle back into sideboard.
Study-desk chair—*not* under desk.
Silver cigarette box—U.L. corner of study desk.
Paper grocer bag with shoes—on floor below desk.

END OF ACT 1—SCENE 2

u. end of chest pulled away from wall.
Hammer—to chest.
Black string with cigarette—pulled to marks—on wall.

CLOSE STUDY DRAPES

Set for Act 1—Scene 3:
Footstool—below R. leg of big throne chair.
Light Sterno in the fireplace.

END OF ACT 1—SCENE 3

Strike:
Newspaper clippings (from sideboard) to off
Electric kettle (from sideboard) to off
Teatray, cups, etc. (from round table) to off.
Grocery bag (from library desk) to off.
Pistols (from library desk)—back to the frames—U.L. study wall.
Bang contraption (from library desk) to off.
Man's shoes (from library desk) to off.
Soda siphon (from stove) to off—then take it to off R.
Dead cigarette (from chest) to off.

Set for Act 1—Scene 4:
2 books (from sideboard) to round table.
Footstool to green marks.
Small throne chair to R. of library desk.
u. library-desk chair—against wall.
David's coat on u. library-desk chair—thrown over back.
David's knapsack to seat of library-desk chair.
Story to library desk.
Silver cigarette box (from library desk) to study desk.

All pistols (from bag on library desk) back to the wall.
Bicycle—on terrace—showing through L. window.
OPEN STUDY DRAPES

END OF ACT 1—SCENE 4
(*End of Act 1*)

Strike:

Books (from round table) to off.
Glass (from round table) to off.
Books (from library desk) to off.
Map (from library desk) to off.
Roll blotter (from library desk) to off.
Attache case (from library desk) to off.
Portable typewriter (from study desk) to off L.
Sterno and burnt paper (from fireplace) to off.

Set for Act 2—Scene 1

Thin leather briefcase (from library desk) with red file inside case
    —R. drawer of desk—unzipped.
Gray paper envelope—on top of briefcase—in drawer.
Soda siphon to sideboard.
Footstool back to scene one marks.
Small throne chair R. of desk—moved D.
U. library-desk chair—angled in
Ornament (from sideboard) to round table.
Bang contraption—properly rigged—gun and cigarette behind chest.
Hammer to desk.
Study-desk chair to between stove and chest.
Battle axe on study-desk chair.
Reload silencer pistol.
Both suitcases (from hall) to off L.

CLOSE STUDY DRAPES.

CLOSE LIBRARY DRAPES TO MARK.

END OF ACT 2—SCENE 1

Strike:

Soda siphon (from sideboard) to off—empty most of soda.
Picture (from sideboard) to off.
Hammer (from chest) to off.

Set for Act 2—Scene 2:

Pile of mail with list of securities in long envelope—on top. D. of U.R. door

Right big throne chair—to green marks.

Small chair below library desk to red marks—D.R.

Bowl of flowers to round table

Dust sheet over: D.R. small chair.

Dust sheet over: R. big throne chair.and round table

Dust sheet over: small chair R. of library desk.

Dust sheet over: library desk and U. library-desk chair.

Study-desk chair—away from desk—*un*swiveled.

Battle axe—back to the L. wall above chest.

OPEN LIBRARY DRAPES.

CLOSE STUDY DRAPES.

SET SHUTTERS OVER LIBRARY WINDOWS.

END OF ACT 2—SCENE 2

Strike:

Dust sheets to off.

Mail and thin briefcase (from library desk) to off.

Red file (from library desk) to off.

Candelabra (from study desk) to off.

Pistols *and* frames (from wall)to off—except silencer which goes to D. bottom desk drawer.

Set for Act 2—Scene 3:

Library desk to red marks.

U. desk chair—to the R. of library desk—set at an angle.

Small chair R. of library desk—moved to the L. of the desk.

David's books, papers, etc. to library desk.

List of securities—library desk.

Julie's glasses—study desk—with case.

Typewriter—study desk—zipped shut.

Typed papers—study desk—U. of typewriter.

Silencer-pistol—D. bottom drawer of study desk.

Fern to brass urn on round table.

Julie's suitcase in hall

OPEN STUDY DRAPES.

STRIKE LIBRARY SHUTTERS.

END OF ACT 2—SCENE 3
(End of Act II)

Strike:

Tray with coffee pot (from sideboard) to off R.—add clean cup ready
  for Act 3—Scene 2
David's papers, books (from library desk) to off.
List of securities (from library desk) to off.
Tray with supper, bottles, cup, snifter, etc. (from lib. desk) to off.
Red file and map (from library desk) to off.
All matches from the library to off!!!!!!
Typewriter (above study desk) to off.

Set for Act 3—Scene 1:

Ash tray—u. end of library desk.
Empty match box—library desk.
Telephone—D.R. end of library desk.
Papers and envelopes—library desk.
Pad and pencil—library desk.
Study-desk chair moved to between chest and stove.
u. end of chest—pulled out from the wall.
Clive's 3 letters on top of study desk—D.L. end; large gray envelope on
  the bottom.
Cloth grocery bag—on floor—below study desk.
Large man's shoes—on floor—below study desk.
Battle axe—u. end of study desk—leaning against wall.
Hammer—on chest.
Almost empty siphon bottle—on chest.
Silencer from study-desk drawer back to frame on U.L. wall.
3 pistols and frames to U.L. wall.
Small tin of fresh cement—terrace.
Trowel—terrace.
White gloves—terrace.
Move brandy bottle from sideboard to off L. prop-table.
Check that newspaper stays in study wastebasket.

CLOSE STUDY DRAPES.

END OF ACT 3—SCENE 1
Strike:

Brandy bottle (from library round table) to off.
Siphon (from sideboard) to off.
Sherry glass (from library desk) to off.
Glass (from study desk) to off.
Rug (from study) to off.

Set for Act 3—Scene 2:

Small chair R. of desk to green marks.
Open library drapes.
Close study door.
Rug with blood to study floor.
Spray water on terrace.

LIBRARY DRAPES OPEN.

COSTUMES

DAVID:

Act 1—Scene 1
Brown tweed jacket
Charcoal slacks
White shirt
Silk red and blue necktie
Gray socks
Tan duffle coat with parka
Brown shoes

Act 1—Scene 2
Takes off jacket and puts on:
Black and gray long sleeve pullover sweater.

Act 1—Scene 3—same as Act 1—Scene 2.

Act 1—Scene 4—same as Act 1—Scene 1.

Act 2—Scene 1—same as Act 1—Scene 1.

Act 2—Scene 2
Brown, tan and green suit with red line check—single breasted.
White shirt.
Red and blue paisley necktie
Same brown shoes
Same gray socks
Trench coat.

Act 2—Scene 3
Removes trench coat.

Act 3—Scene 1—same as Act 2—Scene 2.

Act 3—Scene 2
Removes suit jacket and puts on: brown checked bathrobe.

CLIVE:

Act 1—Scene 1
Green tweed suit—single breasted.
Chocolate waistcoat
Brown suede shoes

93

White shirt
Green silk tie
Gray socks

Act 2—Scene 3

Medium gray suit—single breasted
Light cream waistcoat
White shirt
Blue and gold striped necktie
Same shoes and socks

Act 3—Scene 1—same as Act 2—Scene 3.

JULIE:

Act 1—Scene 1

Two-piece dark olive suit
Dark olive coat
Silk white and brown paisley scarf
Dark green velour tam
Tan purse
Brown walking shoes
Tan pigskin gloves

Act 1—Scene 2

Cinnamon dress
Light brown coat
Dark brown shoes
Same tan purse and gloves as in Act 1—Scene 1.

Act 1—Scene 3—same as Act 1—Scene 2.

Act 1—Scene 4

Dark brown dress with white and brown scarf
Same dark olive coat as Act 1—Scene 1
Same gloves as in earlier scenes
Same purse as in earlier scenes
Same shoes as in Act 1—Scene 2 and Act 1—Scene 3.

Act 2—Scene 1

Green velvet dress
Same shoes as Act 1—Scene 2, Act 1—Scene 3, Act 1—Scene 4
Gold necklace
Gold bracelet

Act 2—Scene 2

Black and white skirt

Trench coat
Brown and gray head scarf
Navy blue purse
Navy blue shoes

Act 2—Scene 3

Adds black and white suit jacket
Black tam
Gray gloves
Black purse
Same shoes as Act 2—Scene 2
Black rain coat

Act 3—Scene 2

Coral rose suit
Black opera pumps
Same black purse as Act 2—Scene 3
Same black rain coat as Act 2—Scene 3
Beige gloves
Black hat

Dr. Woolley:

Act 1—Scene 1

Red and black plaid suit
Matching hat
Brown walking shoes
Tan blouse
Blue striped necktie
Black gloves

Act 2—Scene 1

Brown and black silk print dress
Tan beads
Tan coat
Tan print head scarf
Light brown pumps
Black gloves

Act 3—Scene 1

Same as Act 1—Scene 1 except:
Blue and red striped tie.

Scotland Yard Men:

Act 3—Scene 2

Dark blue overcoats

Black hats
White shirts
Neckties
Dark slacks
Black shoes

CHARLES:

Act 1—Scene 1

Dark blue suit with small stripes—double breasted.
Tan shirt
Blue knit tie
Black shoes—grey socks
White pocket handkerchief
Dark blue overcoat—gray homburg

Act 1—Scene 2

Brown tweed suit
Darker brown waistcoat
Same tan shirt—blue necktie—gray socks
White pocket handkerchief
Brown loafers
Brown tweed overcoat—tan cap

Act 1—Scene 3

Changes to red socks

Act 1—Scene 4

Tan sport shirt—red silk scarf
Brown flannel trousers
Same brown tweed overcoat—tan cap.
    takes off:
Overcoat, cap and scarf
    puts on:
Red sports jacket—red knit necktie
Violet pocket handkerchief

POLICE CONSTARLE:

Act 3—Scene 1

Black rubber coat with cape attached.
Dark blue police suit—silver buttons—silver braid at cuffs
Dark blue police helmet with insignia
Black gloves
Hightop black shoes

MR. TIBBIT:

Act 1—Scene 2
Olive drab corduroy jacket
Olive drab cotton slacks
Brown work shoes
Plaid brown-blue shirt

Act 1—Scene 3—same as Act 1—Scene 2.

NEW PLAYS

★ **RABBIT HOLE by David Lindsay-Abaire.** Winner of the 2007 Pulitzer Prize. Becca and Howie Corbett have everything a couple could want until a life-shattering accident turns their world upside down. "An intensely emotional examination of grief, laced with wit." *—Variety.* "A transcendent and deeply affecting new play." *—Entertainment Weekly.* "Painstakingly beautiful." *—BackStage.* [2M, 3W] ISBN: 978-0-8222-2154-8

★ **DOUBT, A Parable by John Patrick Shanley.** Winner of the 2005 Pulitzer Prize and Tony Award. Sister Aloysius, a Bronx school principal, takes matters into her own hands when she suspects the young Father Flynn of improper relations with one of the male students. "All the elements come invigoratingly together like clockwork." *—Variety.* "Passionate, exquisite, important, engrossing." *—NY Newsday.* [1M, 3W] ISBN: 978-0-8222-2219-4

★ **THE PILLOWMAN by Martin McDonagh.** In an unnamed totalitarian state, an author of horrific children's stories discovers that someone has been making his stories come true. "A blindingly bright black comedy." *—NY Times.* "McDonagh's least forgiving, bravest play." *—Variety.* "Thoroughly startling and genuinely intimidating." *—Chicago Tribune.* [4M, 5 bit parts (2M, 1W, 1 boy, 1 girl)] ISBN: 978-0-8222-2100-5

★ **GREY GARDENS book by Doug Wright, music by Scott Frankel, lyrics by Michael Korie.** The hilarious and heartbreaking story of Big Edie and Little Edie Bouvier Beale, the eccentric aunt and cousin of Jacqueline Kennedy Onassis, once bright names on the social register who became East Hampton's most notorious recluses. "An experience no passionate theatergoer should miss." *—NY Times.* "A unique and unmissable musical." *—Rolling Stone.* [4M, 3W, 2 girls] ISBN: 978-0-8222-2181-4

★ **THE LITTLE DOG LAUGHED by Douglas Carter Beane.** Mitchell Green could make it big as the hot new leading man in Hollywood if Diane, his agent, could just keep him in the closet. "Devastatingly funny." *—NY Times.* "An out-and-out delight." *—NY Daily News.* "Full of wit and wisdom." *—NY Post.* [2M, 2W] ISBN: 978-0-8222-2226-2

★ **SHINING CITY by Conor McPherson.** A guilt-ridden man reaches out to a therapist after seeing the ghost of his recently deceased wife. "Haunting, inspired and glorious." *—NY Times.* "Simply breathtaking and astonishing." *—Time Out.* "A thoughtful, artful, absorbing new drama." *—Star-Ledger.* [3M, 1W] ISBN: 978-0-8222-2187-6

DRAMATISTS PLAY SERVICE, INC.
440 Park Avenue South, New York, NY 10016 212-683-8960 Fax 212-213-1539
postmaster@dramatists.com www.dramatists.com

WRITE ME A MURDER
by Frederick Knott

7M, 2W

Set in Rodingham Manor, an ancient but rather run-down stately house of England, there are two Rodingham brothers, sons of the lord of the manor who wastes no time in dying offstage of natural causes. There is a blunt old party in tweeds, the family doctor, a woman, peppery in a healthy English way. There is shrewd, ruthless, self-made Charles Sturrock who knows where the main commercial chances lie. In addition, there is his appealing young wife, Julie, who would like to be a writer and has a way with character. David Rodingham is a writer whose forte is plot. Intent on wheeling and dealing in land values, Sturrock finds it useful to encourage David to help his wife write a tale about murder. The collaborators are attracted not only to letters but also to romantic ideas, and the seemingly unaware Sturrock at one point assists in dreaming up a perfect crime. Clive Rodingham, the older brother, is something of a playboy. As the heir, he sells the manor to Sturrock and takes off for an heiress in Texas. The plot then thickens as he returns minus wife and funds.

"… as neat a tying-up of clues, hints, deeds and misdeeds as the probing mystery fan could ask." **—The New York World-Telegram & Sun**

"… builds steadily, amusingly and suspensefully and reaches a swift and convincing climax." **—The New York Times**

"… continuously interesting in the twists and curlicues of its plot." **—New York Women's Wear Daily**

Also by Frederick Knott
DIAL "M"
WAIT UN

ISBN 978-0-8222-1279-9

9 780822 212799

90000

DRAMATISTS PLAY SERVICE, INC.